SHHH!
IT'S THE PRINCIPAL
by
Lamar Dodson

Cypress House
Fort Bragg, California

Address all inquiries to the publisher:
  Cypress House
  155 Cypress Street
  Fort Bragg, CA 95437

Citations from *The Principalship: New Perspectives* by Jacobson, Logsdon and Wiegman © 1973. Reprinted by permission of Prentice Hall, Englewood Cliffs, NJ.

Book production by Comp-Type, Inc., Fort Bragg, CA

Manufactured in the U.S.A.

ISBN No. 1-879384-05-1
Library of Congress No. 91-70634

TO MY STAFF

(MY FAMILY AWAY FROM HOME)

ACKNOWLEDGMENTS

I would like to thank a number of people who provided encouragement and assistance to me in the writing of this book. First, I must thank my wife who consistently supports everything I do so enthusiastically.

I also need to acknowledge the editing assistance provided by Mrs. Terry McCullough, a parent who sent two children through Stanislaus School, a school board member, and a good friend. Mrs. Elaine Kline, my mother-in-law, also assisted by providing editing assistance and sharing anecdotes. Her father was a high school principal in the 1920's and a county superintendent in South Dakota.

I owe thanks to Prentice Hall Publishing Company for (*The Principalship: New Perspectives*, 1973) a major portion of Chapter 2 which deals with the early history of the principalship in America.

A final word of thanks to my co-workers at Stanislaus Union Elementary School who may discover themselves in these pages. And of course, I must thank the children who have attended schools in the district where I have served as principal. Without them there would be no book.

Scripture quotations are from the New International version of the Bible, published by the B.B. Kirkbride Bible Company and the Zondervan Corp., copyright 1983.

C O N T E N T S

PREFACE

Many years ago when I was teaching English at a junior high school I kept a journal of sayings, remarks, and stories students recorded in their compositions or their contributions to oral discussions. This turned into quite a collection. The collection was lost when the basement where my things were stored was flooded. That was a devastating blow. It just about wiped out any ambition I had to write a book. This year I decided the time had come, so I began to write about some of the amusing events that have occurred during my career.

A principal does not have an easy job. There are many unpleasant experiences associated with the role of principal. It has been my purpose to relate positive experiences and share helpful ideas. At times you will laugh as you read about the children. I hope you will gain a better understanding of the principal's role in education. If you are a beginning principal, you might find an idea or two that will be useful. If you are a teacher, perhaps you will glean a few insights to help you better understand your principal. And, if you are a parent, perhaps you will learn that your child's personality at school is sometimes quite different than at home. To you Stanislaus parents, I give you my word that I will never reveal to a living soul if it was your children who were referred to in the book. All of the children's names have been changed, and my secretary doesn't even know who they are, and if she doesn't know, no one does.

I have been fortunate during my career as an administrator

to work for a school district which focuses on children and their needs as its number one priority. The governing board of my school district, though members have changed over the years, has provided a quality educational program for children and has supported teachers and administrators alike by giving us the freedom to teach and the encouragement we need to do our job. Many school districts today have problems which include poor teacher/staff morale, lack of fiscal responsibility, inadequate or antiquated curriculum materials, insufficient space to house children, and/or hassles with bargaining units. Not so in this district! It has given me a great deal of satisfaction to be a principal in the Stanislaus Union School District.

It is my hope that you will enjoy reading the amusing anecdotes, learn from the lessons and moral imperatives, and find value in the ideas presented for running a good school.

1

ROOKIE PRINCIPAL

It was the first day of school and, to set the tone for my administration, I arrived bright and early at 6:30 a.m. Not even the custodian was there. Stanislaus Union Elementary School was locked tight, so I had to wait on the red steps for the custodian. Should I ask for a set of keys? Would they tell me that new principals must first prove themselves before being entrusted with the keys to the kingdom?

As I waited, it occurred to me that perhaps I was out of place. As a college student, I hadn't wanted to be a principal. I wasn't even sure I wanted to teach. What does a principal do, I wondered, aside from discipline wayward pupils? My thoughts were interrupted by the sound of footsteps. Emerging from the fog and darkness of dawn in California's central valley, an elderly but sprightly man approached me. "If you're a salesman, the district office is down the road about a mile or so, but there won't be anyone there for at least another hour."

"Actually, I'm the new principal, but I hope you don't need proof. I haven't been given any keys yet."

He looked me up and down the way he might assess a student he was considering for blackboard duty. I guess I passed muster because he grunted, told me his name was

Norman, and, without waiting for me to respond, said, "Follow me." He led me into the main building, where he switched off the burglar alarm and unlocked the shaved glass door which led to the office. "In there," he said. "I can't stay and talk. I've too much to do, and not much time to do it in. Opel—she's your secretary—will be along about quarter past seven, and I reckon she'll tell you where everything is."

I thought about firing him but thanked him instead and groped along the wall for the lightswitch. Well, I was inside. That was a start. Now what? I'd already met Opel and most of the staff in December before winter recess. My new principal's office was about three times larger than the one which had been my home away from home for the previous three years. A large desk, pushed up against one wall in the corner of the room, caught my attention. It was piled high with all sorts of things—a note from my predecessor wishing me good luck, governing board agendas, notes from teachers requesting textbooks or other materials, and stacks and stacks of mail. I spent the next thirty minutes sorting through the "stuff" and filing most of it in the circular file.

At 7:35 a.m. I decided to venture out. I walked out of the office and proceeded in the direction of the Staff Lounge. I had not yet taken up the vice of coffee drinking. Coffee is to administrators as peanuts are to elephants. It wasn't long before I too became a coffee drinker. I thought I might find some hot chocolate. A youngster about ten years old came running up to me shouting that the bus driver requested my presence. I had been discovered. As I hurried out the door toward the bus area, the custodian met me with two very frightened young ladies in tow.

"I caught these two swinging from the partitions in the restroom," he panted. "What do you want me to do with them?"

I had a few ideas. "Let the punishment fit the crime," came to mind. These girls might enjoy writing an essay on "The

Dangers Involved in Restroom Gymnastics." Actually, this would be more appropriate than writing one hundred times "I will not swing from the partitions in the girls' restroom." This practice of "repetition writing" has been used for years but is not very effective in changing behavior. Perhaps the girls would think before swinging if they were given the task of monitoring the restrooms for a few days to make sure other students didn't become swingers.

I told the girls to sit in the hallway and wait until I returned. I continued on my way to the bus area, and boarded the bus in question. There I met a rather upset driver. Andy, the driver, related that one student had stuck his foot out and tripped another student. A scuffle had ensued with Andy being caught in the middle. It seemed reasonable to me that citations should be written for both offenders. I delegated that duty to Andy since it was his bus. I assured him that he could take the time to write the citations, that he definitely had the power to do so, and I would support him when the parents called.

In five minutes I had learned that I was expected "to do something," to have quick and ready answers, and to be everywhere at once. Welcome to Stanislaus Union Elementary School. We're so glad you are with us! Three buses pulled in, off-loaded children, and quickly departed. It's amazing to me that buses can be unloaded so quickly at the beginning of a day or following a field trip, and yet it seems to take forever to load the buses for children to leave after school.

The playground was full of children, and it wasn't even eight o'clock. Bus schedules play a major role in determining life at school. Armed with this information, I was not overly surprised when I discovered that the school day could not begin until 8:30. I quickly learned that the teachers' work day begins at 8:00 a.m., and "Thou shalt not" assign teachers duties before that hour. I spent the next forty-five minutes on the playground. It didn't seem to be a very friendly place. I talked with some children and learned a few names. The bell rang and it seemed like thousands of little bodies rushed past me toward the classrooms. I had survived my first morning recess duty.

When I came into the building after recess, I suddenly remembered that I had told two little girls to sit in the hallway and wait for me. Almost an hour had elapsed. They were scared before. They were petrified now. What would this new principal do to them? I simply told them I was disappointed in their behavior, and I sincerely hoped it would not be necessary for me to contact their parents to suggest that they allow the girls to do more swinging at home. When I dismissed them to go to class, they looked startled, giggled, turned and walked down the hall loudly exhaling air.

Opel, the secretary, whom I had met only briefly, had overheard my discussion with the girls and quickly let me know that I probably should have made more of an example of them. I wondered if hanging them from the flag pole would be appropriate. I soon learned that Opel was efficient, well-organized, and a stickler for detail. She probably knew my job (and everyone else's) better than I did. She would certainly keep me on track. It was also apparent that everything I did or said would be compared to what the previous principal had done or said, and I "had better measure up really fast."

Stanislaus was a small school. I had been informed by the previous principal that there were no discipline problems. This was certainly good news to me since I had been working as a vice principal at one of the district schools which was on double sessions and where I spent my days counseling seemingly endless streams of students referred to me with behavior problems. In educational circles the vice principal is known as "The Hammer." How right could the previous principal be when two "discipline" problems (that's what I called them at the other school) had already come to my attention before school even began on the first day after winter break?

The former principal was a fun-loving fellow who was well-respected by the staff, parents, and children in this rural, farming community. I knew I had a hard act to follow! He had been assigned and given time to open a new district elementary school which would be completed in March. In the picture which he had painted for me I had visions of the principal sitting behind his desk with feet propped up, reading the newspaper, and drinking endless cups of coffee. Rumor had it around the district that the closest thing to a discipline problem occurred when one of the children in a fit of anger called another child a "nerd." And then there was the time someone was overheard by a teacher saying "darn." I soon learned this image had been grossly over-exaggerated.

I determined that I would be myself. Those with whom I worked would have to accept me as I was. This was a veteran staff. Nine of the thirteen teachers at the school were rapidly approaching retirement age. I had some ideas which I was eager to try, but I recognized that change is difficult to accomplish even under the best of circumstances, and it certainly would not be wise for a new principal to begin with a lot of changes. I decided to "test the water" at my first faculty meeting that afternoon. I announced to the teachers that I would like to start a Student Council. I had been the adviser for the Student Council at our junior high school and felt that a student government at the elementary level would provide valuable leadership training for youngsters. The idea met immediate resistance.

"Oh, we had a Student Council here once but it fizzled," volunteered one intermediate teacher.

Another responded, "You can try it if you want, but teachers don't have time to work with a Student Council."

I boldly announced that I planned to be the Student Council Adviser and that all I asked was for them to elect two representatives from each third through sixth grade class to come to the scheduled meetings. I sensed that there was "sort of" a consensus by the faculty, and I happily accepted it as a major victory.

This bold venture into student government at the elementary level was met with enthusiastic support by parents. Students were elected by classmates to serve a one-semester term of office. Council members learn parliamentary procedure and conduct their business according to guidelines established in their by-laws and constitution. Over the years the Council has greatly enhanced the physical environment of the campus by their fund-raising drives. Officers conduct monthly meetings, assist the principal at assemblies, and share ideas and problems from their classmates on ways to improve the school. Participating on the Student Council teaches students to be responsible. They take responsibility and learn how to be leaders. They gain a better understanding of themselves and learn to be patient with the sometimes slow-moving process of democratic government.

Following the meeting, I adjourned to my office to reflect on my adventures during this first day of "being the Principal." The two discipline cases that day were minor in comparison to what I was accustomed to handling. It was almost time to go home, and I had yet to speak with an angry parent! The superintendent had not called to relay a message from a parent who "went straight to the top," and I had managed to get through the day without a delegation of teachers waiting to see me about the lack of teaching materials in their classrooms. I determined that it might even be possible for me to take a lunch break at this school (a luxury I seldom experienced before).

I was concerned about the lack of friendliness I had experienced from both staff and students. Everyone seemed so intense. In later years I was introduced to the statement, "Are we having fun yet?" For the most part persons at this school definitely were not having fun, and it was not much fun for me that first day. I reminded myself that it was January (not the most sparkling month of the year), Christmas had just passed, vacation was over, staff and students had just lost a principal they loved dearly, and what could they possibly have to cheer about with a new rookie principal they would have to "break in."

2

PRINCIPALS THEN AND NOW

In the olden days principals as we know them now did not exist. American schools in the 1800's were usually one-room structures. In larger villages sometimes there were two rooms. One teacher was generally in charge of children who attended the one-room schoolhouse. There was no principal. In areas which had more children attending schools a superintendent administered the affairs of the school and supervised the teachers.

The Stanislaus School site was the location of one of the first schools in this district. It was a typical white, one-room structure which occupied the space where the multi-purpose room is now located. It is interesting to read the minutes of mothers' club meetings dating back to the 1940's, and to look through the scrapbooks of old pictures and memorabilia collected by the ladies in this organization. From time to time I have displayed some of this information on the bulletin boards in the hallway. Parents and visitors enjoy viewing this display while waiting to see me or to pick up their children for medical or dental appointments. Once in awhile parents or visitors will recognize one of their friends or an old timer still living in the community. There really isn't a great deal of information in print about early schools. Even less information exists about principals. If the early principals were as busy as principals are today, it is easy to understand why there is not much literature about the evolution of the principalship.

The high school principalship is the oldest administrative position in American education. Early principals were known as masters or head teachers. It is commonly known that teachers in America during early American history were not considered professionals. The first principalships were not considered to be professional positions either. The duties of the master or principal were extremely varied. In addition to teaching and administering his school, the principal often served as town clerk, church chorister, official visitor of the sick, bell ringer of the church, grave digger, and court messenger.* Vice principals and perhaps some principals today will relate to the "messenger" role. Many of us have felt that the principal is a "gofer."

As the population of the United States grew in the 1800's there was a dramatic increase in the number of elementary schools. Superintendents could no longer do it all. Head teachers were selected by superintendents to be responsible for the organization of the school, to oversee the curriculum, to supervise teachers, and to discipline students. Often friction developed between the head teacher and other teachers at the school. The job description for an early elementary school principal might look something like the following:

The head teacher will:

1. Function as the head of the school charged to his care.
2. Regulate the classes and course of instruction of all the pupils, whether they occupied his room or the rooms of other teachers.

---

*Paul B. Jacobson, "The Principal and the Principalship," The Principalship: New Perspectives (1973), pp 28.

3. Discover any defects in the school and apply remedies.
4. Make defects known to the trustee of the ward or district if he could not remedy the conditions.
5. Give necessary instruction to his assistants.
6. Classify pupils.
7. Safeguard school houses and furniture.
8. Keep the school clean.
9. Refrain from impairing the standing of assistants, especially in the eyes of their pupils.
10. Require the cooperation of his assistants.*

Later in the middle of the nineteenth century, the job description for the principalship in large cities revealed that the controlling head of the school was a teaching male principal. Primary grades or departments had women principals under the direction of the male principal. The principal had prescribed duties which were limited largely to discipline, routine administrative acts, and grading pupils in the various rooms.

Early principals were always expected to teach. How did we ever stray from that concept? It has merit! When I was first employed in the district in the 1960's, a teaching vice principal assisted the principal at the junior high level. This person was required to teach during the morning session. He was then released during the afternoon to perform administrative duties. Principals today often "fill in" for teachers when no substitute teachers are available. Principals who continue to teach tend to show more empathy for their teachers. Administrators are often accused by the teaching staff of not understanding how it really is in their world. Several years ago Stanislaus School piloted a "More Able Learner" program. This pilot program was to become the forerunner of the

*Jacobson, The Principalship:, pp. 29-30.

district's gifted and talented program which is now housed at another district school. This successful pilot program provided me with a natural opportunity to teach. The staff had in-service training, attended conferences, workshops, and conventions to become familiar with effective teaching skills to utilize with gifted students.

Principals during the early 1900's began to gain some prestige. The central office delegated more responsibilities to the principal. He gained the right to decide which pupils should be promoted, could transfer and assign teachers, and was given more responsibility for buildings and grounds.* The principal whom I succeeded made the rounds to be sure all of the windows and doors at the site were securely locked. There are lots of windows and doors! Early principals would turn over in their graves if they knew that principals now delegate that responsibility to the custodial staff. Modern principals are generally relieved of direct responsibility for the school plant. As schools have grown in size, so have central offices. And with the increase have come added personnel such as business managers, personnel directors, and maintenance supervisors.

Early principals had little or no time to perform supervisory functions. Even today administrative duties tend to occupy the major portion of the principal's time in most school districts. The district superintendent was expected to oversee the improvement of instruction. If he did not perform this function, it was not done at all. The Stanislaus Union School District has taken a stand and established the improvement of instruction as a priority. All of the teachers in the district have been trained to use effective teaching techniques. By using these techniques our good teachers have become even better. Each year newly hired teachers also receive this training. Principals observing in our classrooms routinely see many of

---

*Jacobson, *The Principalship*, pp 31-2.

the elements of effective teaching strategies being utilized. These routine strategies include providing an anticipatory set, motivational techniques, giving directions, guided practice, reinforcement, questioning, using "sponge activities," and evaluation. Principals have been trained in clinical supervisory techniques so that they can effectively evaluate instructional programs. The focus of the district is clearly to improve instruction, and it is the principal's responsibility to bring that about.

It is fair to characterize supervision by the principal before 1900 as inspection.* He was affectionately known as the "snoopervisor." He visited classrooms, but the focus of the evaluation he wrote on the teacher centered on the physical condition and appearance of the classroom, the teacher's voice level and control, proper ventilation, and perhaps quizzing pupils to be sure they were learning something.† Unfortunately, some principals are still locked into this approach to supervision.

Normal schools in early America provided teacher training. As school populations increased and superintendents were no longer able to do everything, successful teachers often became teaching masters or principals. This practice has not changed until recent years. Coaches were often promoted to the principalship because of their ability to maintain discipline. Many graduate schools of education now offer training for men and women who desire to make the principalship a career. Demonstrating competence in the classroom and/or maintaining order are no longer considered sufficient qualifications for being a principal.

Qualifications necessary for being a successful principal include the ability to organize, to be able to administer his school without allowing it to consume his time, to have time

*Ibid., p. 33.
†Ibid.

to supervise instruction, to be a wise and discreet executive who handles parents with tact, firmness, and skill, and to be able to make decisions promptly and correctly.* He will also need the ability to delegate responsibility when possible. He must be a good business manager. In many districts today the principal oversees the site budget, school improvement budget, student body account, student store, field trip expenses, and serves as an advisor to the parent group in spending money earned by that group. One qualification which cannot be assumed by districts selecting new principals is the candidate's own competence to teach. Other desirable qualities for a principal to be successful include good health, a high degree of intelligence, and personal charm. An even temper is an asset for anyone who deals with the public and who is in constant contact with children. Hopefully, early principals who were dictatorial, pompous, and brash in nature are a thing of the past.

Today principals must be "jacks-of-all-trades" as the following list humorously demonstrates.

SO YOU'RE A PRINCIPAL!

Besides the usual qualifications and proper degrees you need:

- a steady hand and a steadier head
  a sense of humor
- alligator hide—to take the buffs and rebuffs
  sympathy—for the big and petty problems
- knowledge—for what is going on inside and outside of the school
- availability—to be in the office at all times and willing to "stop in the middle" for everyone
- public relations—the oil of good feeling between

---

*ibid.

teachers, employees, parents, and the public
- discipline—for students and teachers
- planning—looking ahead
- flexibility—to take over a class, give a speech, appease a parent—even without a moment's notice
- love—of the job and all it entails
- enjoyment—of the whole "shebang"
- dedication—to do one's best despite setbacks
- firmness and insistence—to get things accomplished
- memory—to remember everything that others forget
- cheerfulness—at all times
- decisions—decisions—decisions
- patience—of a saint to listen to everyone's gripes
- courage—to carry on with very few bouquets

In the past principals were content with the status quo. They made few demands, followed orders from the central office, and did their job without questioning. Principals in most districts still do not enjoy tenure as teachers do. Principals generally must possess a master's degree although an additional stipend is not granted them for advanced degrees. Teachers receive additional pay for units and degrees earned above their bachelor's degree. Many principal organizations are increasing in power and effectiveness today. Higher salaries are paid to principals now. They work a longer day and year than teachers.

Effective superintendents today are providing excellent leadership to districts. They are encouraging school boards to recognize the importance of proper utilization of the principal in the schools. Schools in America will greatly improve when school boards and central office personnel provide administrative assistants and clerical help to principals. Principals should not be required to requisition and distribute supplies, stamp books, do and see that clerical work is done, answer the telephone, or supervise the work of custodians.

These duties are important; however, the primary role of the principal in schools today should be the improvement of instruction.

Selected References

Jacobson, Paul B., James D. Logsdon, and Robert R. Wiegman, "The Principal and the Principalship," *The Principalship: New Perspectives.* New Jersey: Prentice-Hall, Inc., 1973, 28-48.

3

SHHH! IT'S THE PRINCIPAL

I was trying to remember when a principal ever came into the classroom during my school years. I'm sure there must have been a time or two, perhaps more, but I don't remember a single time. In contrast, today's principal is constantly in the classroom. In my district, principals visit classrooms regularly. I know of one district where principals are required to spend up to one-half of their working day directly involved with teachers by either being in their classrooms or interacting with them in the educational process. That is quite a commitment but is certainly the way it should be.

In years past, teachers and students dreaded to face the principal. He was in a position of authority. No one wanted to see "The Man." Until recent years, he could paddle students who misbehaved. He had the last word and, as a student or teacher, one did not dare talk back to him. I have purposely used the masculine pronoun because in those "olden" days, there were far more men serving as principals than women. The trend has definitely changed in recent years.

There are still vestiges of the harsh-type character in the principal's role today. It seems that most of them were well known by staff and students for being harsh, demeaning, and abusive. I sincerely hope that my experience was not typical. I have served as vice principal and/or principal of three schools, and the initial expectation of the person in the principal's role has been the same at each school. When I called a student to the office, that person's first thought was that he/she was in trouble. When I was a vice principal, many times that was the case. You could almost see RELIEF written on the person's face when he/she discovered that there was another purpose for the visit besides being "chewed out."

My second teaching assignment was in a small town in south Texas at a school with over 900 Latin American students. The principal of the school was a former Navy Commander, and he ran the school like a ship. His reputation preceded him. All the rumors I had heard were true. Teachers and students alike were afraid of him. I had began my teaching career with a fourth grade migrant class in November of the previous year at another school in this district composed of all Anglo-Saxon, clean-cut kids from middle income families.

When school commenced the following September, I was one of several new teachers at the school. There was a long, covered corridor with wide sidewalks running along each wing of the school. Each of the classrooms had large glass windows that opened up to the corridor. I have vivid memories of the principal walking down these corridors in military fashion. I lived in fear and trembling at the thought that he could come into my classroom at any time to evaluate my teaching. I knew my fears had some basis in fact when I heard that the principal had walked into a new female teacher's classroom to observe. She took one look at him as he seated himself in back of the room with his clipboard (clipboards were invented for principals!) and fainted dead away.

The first year I taught seventh grade English in my present school district brought a similar experience. A second-year physical education teacher who taught across the way from me was being observed by the principal. The teacher was obviously unprepared, and after the health lesson had proceeded for only a few minutes, the embarrassed teacher asked the principal to step outside the door with him. He explained to the principal that he was not having a good day, was very nervous, and could the principal please come back another time. Of course, the principal accepted the offer of a rain check, came back on another day, and everything was fine.

My teachers think nothing of it when I visit their classrooms. It is business as usual. Teachers have more visitors in their rooms now due to both formal and informal site reviews. Many parents also visit school as volunteer helpers or just to spend some time in their child's school environment.

One of my sixth grade teachers who was rarely absent called in sick. He had a very difficult class that year, and I was somewhat relieved when I learned that his substitute was a man who looked like he could have been a starting guard for the San Francisco 49'ers. He was a BIG man! I assumed there would be no problems in the classroom with this man in charge. My school was built in 1956 and, fortunately, was not equipped with an intercom system. Most teachers would agree that these contraptions are one of the seven curses of the education world. Each classroom had an individual handset which worked like a telephone and allowed the teacher and secretary to communicate. This mode of communication is just one notch up from the old tin cans with a string attached or two notches above the smoke signals used by American Indians. A new intercom system has since been installed. Now teachers have open lines to all rooms in the school. The substitute called the office at approximately 10:30 requesting that the principal come to his room. Since he seemed rather anxious and the secretary detected "loud noises" emanating through the headset, she delivered the message to me immediately. I did not have my own headset in those days. That was a real fringe benefit! I rushed to this sixth grade classroom and walked boldly into the room in "take-charge" fashion.

It seems like the older students always have a lookout! Now, it was apparent to the class that the substitute had called the office; however, it was not obvious to them that contact had been made with the principal. There was no way for the students to know if the principal would come. This rather shrewd lookout had been on guard at the window to see if anyone would come to the substitute's rescue. As I walked down the corridor approaching the classroom and just before I reached the door, I heard the lookout shout, "Shhh! It's the principal!" The room became absolutely quiet. I didn't have to say a word. Such power! As the kids say, "It was awesome."

This huge, six-foot-five, 230-pound man hurried up to me with tears streaming down his face and sputtered, "I just can't take it anymore. These kids are terrible! They won't mind. They won't do anything I ask them to do. You'll have to take the class. I'm leaving!"

I calmly suggested that he and I step outside the door and have a chat. I convinced him that it was in his best interest to stick it out for the remainder of the day and I would help him all I could. We went back into the room where I delivered a short, pungent speech. I left the class to the substitute. He made it through the day just fine.

I've heard "Shhh! It's the principal!" many times since that first experience. Most often it has been when the regular teacher was absent. Substitutes have a very difficult role to play, but they do an excellent job under the circumstances.

Just before the winter break one school year, I was walking down the long hallway in Wing A going toward the kinder-garten rooms. As I walked by one of the first grade class-rooms, I heard a teacher comment, "I see Billy thinking."

I took a few more steps before deciding to go back and

check this out. I did an about face and came back to the classroom in question. As I approached the room several thoughts went through my mind. I thought, "Here is a young teacher who has astonishing powers." Or, "The teacher colleges are certainly doing a better job of preparing teachers these days." Both statements are quite probably true.

I stood at the doorway watching for a few moments. Evidently, Billy or another student was called on to answer the "thinking" question. Either that or there was much thinking going on in the room and I just wasn't blessed with the powers to perceive it happening. After all, this was a first grade classroom. Now, in a fifth or sixth grade, I'm quite sure that even I would be able to see the thinking going on there. I think!

Sensing that this was a talent worthy of sharing with others, I asked the teacher how it was that she was able to detect children thinking. Being the astute teacher that she was, she immediately performed a demonstration lesson for me. This new teacher had just completed effective teacher training. In this extensive, three-day in-service she had learned some practical ways to improve instruction. One of the ways teachers may enhance learning is to involve the entire class in the lesson and be able to evaluate instantly to see who has and who has not learned the particular concept. One of the techniques teachers learned, called an "overt" response, has children signal by using a thumbs up/down/sideways sign, place their hands on their head, touch an ear, or use some other visual means of signaling. In this particular instance where the teacher "observed Billy thinking" she had adapted a covert action (thinking) to accompany an overt action (tapping head with fingers) as an evaluation tool and to involve children in the lesson. She asked the class a question and immediately thirty little hands began thumping their heads. All of the children were smiling and glancing around to be sure that I recognized that they were thinking. I'm sure *all* of them were THINKING. What smart kids! What a teacher! What a school! It's a fun place to be, and we get paid for it. A friend of mine who retired a few years ago was hired to play Santa at a local store. He was perfect for the part. He was a REAL Santa! Each day he took his position in a rocking chair at the store's main entrance. Everyone who came into the store passed by him. This store is located in an area close to my school, and many parents of children in my school shop there. Harry, my friend, and I sing in a church choir. At practice he told me about a mother and her little girl who came into the store and stopped by to visit him. In his role as Santa he asked the girl all of the standard questions, and then he asked her where she went to school. When she told him that she was in the second grade at Stanislaus School, Harry made the connection.

He said, in his Santa voice, "Ho, Ho, Ho, I know your principal! He's Lamar Dodson and a pretty good guy. I may even leave him a gift this year."

The very next day after Harry told me about this incident, I was doing some Christmas shopping in a department store across town. A lady whom I did not recognize and her little girl walked by me.

The mother said, "Cindy, that was your principal."

Cindy turned around and ran toward me. She loudly exclaimed, "Santa Claus knows your name!"

I looked around sheepishly to see who was watching. It was my hope that this information wouldn't leak out. "What? Santa knows my name? I can't believe it! How in the world would he know my name? He must know everyone," I replied.

I made a really big deal of it. Cindy was impressed that Santa knew her principal. The next day in the cafeteria she made it a point to speak to me (In fact, she said, "Hi, Lamar" at which time I gave her my "principal look") and to remind me about our mutual friend, Santa.

The most fun I have in life is getting up in the morning and going to school. I enjoy being a principal! I certainly do not relate to the story about the mother who could not get her son up in the morning. The mother knocked on the son's bedroom door telling him it was time to get up and get ready for school. The son was slow in responding. He let his mother know that he had a headache, it was his birthday, and he didn't want to go to school. His mother said, "You have to get out of that bed and go to school, son. I know it's your fortieth birthday and you would rather be playing golf, but you are the principal and they expect you to be at school."

Sure, there are terrible, no-good, downright bad days at school. There are days when I would much rather be sitting in a chaise lounge under the palm trees sipping a Coke by the pool while looking out on the Pacific Ocean on any one of the Hawaiian Islands.

In my high school yearbook for the senior year when the "Predictions" were recorded for those graduating, my class-mates had me pegged as a teacher. Unbelievable! Entering any career related to "school" was out of the question. My childhood days provided no clues in that direction. There were no kindergarten programs in Texas. I missed the cutoff date to begin first grade by six days. I was seven when I was initiated into the school experience. Most boys are better off beginning school later anyway. My elementary school years do not bring back pleasant memories. I would have qualified for every special education program in existence today. In those days the teacher had to cope the best he could with children who spoke no English, those with severe behavior problems, and with those who truly needed special services.

Someone discovered that I couldn't see when I was in second grade. That was the year the teacher kept hitting my knuckles with a ruler because I couldn't spell. I never did figure out how hitting my knuckles would get those words into my head. I also ran into a few trees on the way to school.

We're talking blind. The glasses helped. I didn't run into any more trees. Still, I was propelled through the elementary grades without ever learning how to read. In junior high I finally learned to read. Several teachers took an interest in me during my junior/senior high school years. One teacher even encouraged me to go to college. Radical! No one in my family (five children) had gone to college. I decided to attend Baylor University in Waco, Texas. Baylor is a Baptist, church-supported school. I felt a warm welcome there. Everyone (including professors and students) was so friendly.

Previously I mentioned the cold, unfriendly atmosphere I felt when I first arrived at Stanislaus School. Children did not smile. People did not seem friendly. I suspected that some of the fields surrounding the campus might be producing sour pickles and that the children were eating these before coming to school. No one seemed to enjoy being at school. I wanted the experience I had at Baylor University where everyone was so friendly to repeat itself at Stanislaus.

A wise man is quoted as saying, "We are the product of our experiences." I am the type of leader I have become because of my past experiences. I attend conferences, seminars, workshops, and conventions to gain ideas. When I travel to other cities, I try to visit schools to gather ideas I can bring back to Stanislaus. A superintendent I once worked for shared that if you gain one good idea from a conference, you can consider the experience worthwhile. I have gleaned ideas from others which have been adapted to fit my situation. Every year promises new, exciting challenges.

4

PRINCIPALS DO THE DARNDEST THINGS

One time I interviewed for a vice principal position at a junior high school. There were nine persons on the interview team. This in itself was not significant; however, I had never been before an interview team composed of so many administrators, classified persons, parents, and students. I didn't know what to expect! During the interview an administrator on the team asked me what I would do if two students were involved in a fight just a few feet from me. I thought for a moment and responded that it would all depend on how big the two persons were. Some of the members of the interview team laughed—loudly. I'm not sure if it was my response or their laughter, but the question did not receive any more input from me.

The answer that interviewer was seeking was for the principal to immediately intervene to separate the combatants. Sometimes it is as simple as speaking softly, taking each student by the arm, and asking them to stop. There are times when the principal must forcefully intervene—especially if he determines that the students may hurt each other.

Several persons on the interview team became involved in a heated argument about proper procedure for "breaking up a fight." Evidently the fight situation described had actually happened in a hallway just outside a teacher's door in the presence of the teacher. The principal just happened to be walking by at the time the fight broke out. The teacher had not intervened to stop the fight. It was the teacher's opinion that the principal had the primary responsibility of getting between the two combatants. The principal maintained that it was the teacher's responsibility to stop the fight in any way possible. I'm not sure that anyone won that argument. Needless to say, one of the things principals are called upon to do is mediate fight situations.

It is not my objective to diminish the role of the principal. Most principals are greatly overworked and underpaid. Neither is it my intent to claim that the principal is "above" doing many of the menial tasks which they are required to perform. There are many dedicated, hardworking principals in the field today. I'm not sure our society will ever be willing to compensate educators adequately. School boards and those in top level administrative positions are becoming more aware of the need to allow the principal to be the instructional leader at the school. In many cases assistant principals or administrative aides are hired to take care of many clerical functions. There is definitely room for improvement in the training process of future administrators. Perhaps principal internships need to be required for all persons seeking to become administrators.

Being a vice principal is a good proving ground for future principals. My chores included counting and stamping books; threading 16 mm manual film projectors; moving audio visual equipment from one location to another without dumping it on the sidewalk; monitoring children in the cafeteria as they ate lunch; supervising a detention room full of youngsters who had been referred there by teachers, custodians, bus drivers, yard duty supervisors, and even by the principal; putting on bandaids, blowing a whistle when children run on the sidewalk after the bell rings; conducting the annual furniture and equipment inventory; leading the safety patrol; handling a constant stream of youngsters of all ages who had been referred to the office for all kinds of reasons; being the adviser for the Student Council; taking charge of the annual candy sale; and sitting through three to four hours of meetings without a "potty" break. It is generally accepted that the vice principal who can do all of these things is prepared to be a REAL principal. If you are fortunate enough to become the principal of a small school (under 650 is considered small), you may indeed be a REAL principal and still "get to do" many of these tasks.

The restrooms were not clean. That's a fact. I had let the custodian know that I wanted clean restrooms. Word had also reached the district office that the custodian was not adequately cleaning the restrooms. It was definitely time for top level administrative decision-making to take place. One bright sunny day when everything was under control at the district office, the superintendent came to visit the school. He made a thorough inspection of the not-so-clean restrooms, came to the office, and told the secretary to call for the custodian. He intercepted me as I was returning to my office, and along with the custodian who had now arrived, we proceeded to the restrooms in question. The superintendent looked at the baseboards in the Boys' Restroom and pointed out to the custodian the dirt which had gathered there. The custodian did indeed recognize it as dirt. The superintendent asked the custodian to bring in a pail of water (Was he remembering JACK AND JILL?), a scouring pad, a can of Ajax, and a sponge. Shortly, the custodian returned with these items. The superintendent got down on his knees and began cleaning the dirt from the baseboard.

After he had cleaned a two-foot area, he looked up smugly, smiled at the custodian, and said, "Now that's the way you clean a dirty restroom."

It was so simple! The superintendent had effectively demonstrated that dirt could be easily removed from restroom baseboards by the application of a little elbow grease. Of course, being the astute manager that I was, I knew this was not the problem. The night custodian was required to clean the cafeteria and kitchen, move supplies, clean sixteen classrooms (being allowed only fifteen minutes per room), the hallway, and all of the restrooms throughout the school, deal with interruptions, open the multi-purpose room for night meetings and clean up afterwards, and secure all of the buildings during his eight-hour shift. However, as true as these facts were, an even more important issue was involved. Here was my superintendent taking time to "teach" a custodian how to accomplish a routine job. Was he, in fact, showing me how to do my job too? If it was important enough for the district superintendent to get involved, then surely there wasn't any task too unimportant for me to do as the principal of the school.

One grim reality of the principalship involves dealing with "not enough." School district budgets are never adequate. School boards and district-level administrators constantly deal with ways to prioritize needs. The "crunch" is often felt at the site level. In a small school when adequate custodial time is not provided due to lack of funds, the principal must spend more time supervising custodians. Scheduling regular meetings to discuss time management techniques, prioritizing projects, and general operational concerns is essential. It is also important for the principal to monitor or follow through to make sure tasks are accomplished as directed. Teachers need to cooperate with the custodial staff by leaving their classrooms ready for cleaning. This includes teaching children to be responsible for picking up large pieces of paper, pencils, paper clips, pens or staples which the vacuum cleaner will not take. Children can also stack chairs and keep their desks clean.

I had hired a new sixth grade teacher one year to accommodate a growing population. The teacher was young and right out of college. In her class that year was a rather large boy who might have accurately been labeled "Pigpen" because of his unkempt appearance. None of the children liked to sit near this person. In addition, this rather large boy sometimes had a problem controlling his bladder.

You might ask, "Did you refer the boy to the nurse?" Yes, I did. Several home visits were made by the nurse. Numerous discussions were held between the nurse and the boy. The nurse requested that the family seek medical assistance. All to no avail. One fine, freezing-cold winter day, the teacher called the office and told the secretary that she was sending the boy to the office. She and the class could no longer stand "the smell." It was obvious as the boy walked down the hallway to the office, that immediate attention must be given to this problem. This was not the nurse's day to be at school. The secretary called the boy's home only to be told that the mother had no transportation. She could not come to school to bring clean pants or to take the boy home. What to do? Surely the principal with all of his training and wealth of experience could handle this situation. Bringing all of my decision-making skills to bear, I decided to take the boy home, but not in MY car. The mother gave me verbal permission to transport her son home. The district owned an old Ford pickup truck which had affectionately been named the "Silver Bullet." I secured a set of keys to the truck from the maintenance building and drove the truck to the front of the school. Sitting in the cab with the motor running, I motioned for the boy to join me. Remember, it was a freezing-cold day. The secretary had given me the boy's address, and I noted that we had a fifteen-minute drive ahead of us. There was no heater in the truck. It was really a clunker. I agonized as long as I could and then rolled down the window. I made some comment as I stuck my head out the window about the fog obstructing my vision. Finally, the trip was completed, my passenger delivered safely to his home, and I was on my way back to school with BOTH windows down. I'm not sure the old Silver Bullet was ever the same after that.

A principal should not have to deal with a problem such as this. Society has increasingly given schools more areas to administer. Typically, first grade children must have a physical health examination in order to be admitted to school. No youngsters are permitted to enroll without up-to-date immunization records. Dealing with child neglect and abuse cases takes much time. Children experience varied kinds of health problems (inhalers for allergies, bee sting kits for those who must receive immediate attention from a sting, hyperactivity—to name a few) which require staff training and attention. When the school is not adequately staffed, the principal has to wear many hats. Unless our society comes to grips with the necessity of providing adequate funds for all areas involved in the educational process, this problem will continue.

The district wanted to experiment with a K-8 school concept. It was decided that my school would be perfect for this pilot program. Being the smallest school in the district with slightly less than three hundred students, it was feasible to add a seventh grade class, and if everything went well, to add an eighth grade class the following year. The seventh graders would come from all of the other elementary schools in the district. Students were to be "chosen" for this class with incoming seventh graders from my school being given the first priority. Unfortunately, most of my graduating sixth graders chose to go to the junior high school. A class of eighteen students and a new teacher, who was hired late in August, were ready to go.

One incident during that year which epitomized a frustrating time in my life as a principal occurred on a fine spring day in late May when I was informed by the secretary that the superintendent wished to speak to me on the telephone.

Picking up the receiver, I was greeted with, "Do you need help running that school?"

Well, naturally we all need help from time to time, but I could tell by the tone of his voice that he wasn't trying to be funny. Try, fear! Yes, I think he was trying to produce some measure of fear in me. He succeeded. I asked for an explanation. I figured I might as well know what I was shaking about.

"One of your neighbors across the road called the district office complaining about two of your students who are in their orchard. This has happened before." (Later I checked on this, and sure enough when the school was a junior high school many years before, students constantly cut through this same neighbor's orchard on the way home. It had not happened during the time I had been principal there.) "This behavior will not be tolerated." (Was he talking about me shaking in my boots? How could he know that?) "What are you going to do about it?"

I gulped, took a deep breath, and nervously replied, "I need to know when the boys were there. Are they still in the orchard? Were they confronted? Did they refuse to leave?" I felt that knowing these things would help me make a better decision.

"Those things are immaterial. When I was principal of that school, I did whatever it took to keep things under control. Neighbors did not call the district office to complain about students in my school. If need be I would run into the orchard and chase the students until I caught them," he angrily responded.

Somewhat more controlled, I stated, "I do not feel that it is my job to chase students who run in the orchard. If they were still there, I would call the sheriff. I will call the neighbor and recommend that she call the sheriff if there are further occurrences like this. I will have a serious talk with the two young men in the morning. I will also let their parents know about this misbehavior. If any other action is necessary . . ." (such as a suspension from school if their prior discipline record indicated repeated offenses), "I will take it."

To my knowledge there were no further incidents of children cutting through the orchard. My seventh grade class had a short history. It lasted that one year and was dropped. Incidentally, I have gone into the orchard to bring students out. My school is surrounded by almond orchards. There are almond orchards on all three sides of the playground which is behind the school. In front, a state highway divides the school from still another almond orchard. Once a sixth grade boy became angry at his teacher who had just reprimanded him. He stormed out of the classroom, ran into the orchard, and climbed a tree. The teacher called the office when the student left to alert us. This can be a serious problem for many reasons. The farmer may be spraying his trees with pesticides. The district would be liable if the student damaged the farmer's property. The student might injure himself. And once, a student went into the orchard and could not be found. I called the Sheriff's Department and deputies were dispatched to find the boy. He was located about a mile from the school going toward the city limits. So, I do take it seriously when students are reported in the orchard. I walked out to the orchard and coaxed the boy down out of the tree. We had a friendly chat, and he agreed to go back to class, apologize to the teacher, and take his punishment (which turned out to be a detention after school).

The district I work for is small. It was much smaller when I began teaching seventh grade English at the school where I am presently serving as the principal. I inherited a school with multi-colored classrooms. This was evidently the rage of the age or a perfectly designed experiment based on years of research to study the effects of color on children. Take your pick. Anyway, being the conservative that I am and having been prodded by many teachers, I requested that the classrooms be repainted during the coming summer break. There was no disagreement about the condition of the classrooms. They were badly in need of refurbishing. However, there was no money available to do the job. Rather than face another multi-colored year, I requested that the paint be provided to do the job, and I would provide the labor. Not only did the district provide the paint, they hired a high school senior to assist me. Together that summer we wiped out the colorful environment replacing it with more conservative colors. I must admit that now, thirteen years later, teachers are once again requesting that their rooms be repainted. Are they never satisfied? I told them it was not in my contract. Not really. In this day and age with negotiations being what they are, a certificated employee may not perform work of this nature because it would be taking work from the classified employees' bargaining unit. So, my painting career came to an end.

Sometimes the principal must be a first aid officer. We always encourage students to walk, play safely, respect the rights of others, and all those good rules that just about every school in America has. One boy rather new to the school was running from his classroom which was the last room on the third row of buildings. As he rounded the corner of the second building heading toward the office going full speed, he collided with another student who was walking. I'm not sure about all that transpired before he arrived at the office, but he was a mess. There was so much blood it was difficult to tell how much damage had been done to his teeth. His mother was called and gave the nurse permission to take him to the family dentist. We called the dentist to find out what procedures to follow. He indicated that the two permanent teeth which were knocked out could be re-implanted if brought in soon enough. What teeth? I immediately led a searching party to recover the missing teeth. After scouring the area amidst the blood and spilled books and papers, we found the teeth. The dentist had directed us to keep the teeth moist and transport them to him as quickly as possible. I made haste to deliver the teeth which were successfully reintroduced to the boy's mouth. Boy and teeth did nicely.

About fifteen years ago the Parents Club joined together to completely renovate the playground equipment. On several consecutive weekends with much man (and woman) power, many different types of equipment were built including a huge twelve foot tall tower with stairs on one end and a slide on the other. This square structure had railings around the sides and a fireman's pole to slide down. It was a sight to behold. The first time I saw it, it scared me to death. I imagine it gave small children the same feeling. But, I have to admit that I waited until everyone had gone home one evening, ascended to the top via the stairs, and propelled myself down the slide. Children loved to play tag on it. Unfortunately, sometimes they fell from the top. Even the soft sand below was not enough to prevent injuries. So, the TOWER was removed. Then there were the monkey bars. This very popular piece of playground equipment also contributes a fair share of accident reports. One time I was called to the monkey bar area where a girl lay on the sand in a great deal of pain. She had fallen on her arm which was obviously broken (the bone sticking out was my first clue). After determining that there were no back injuries, we took the girl to the office. I gingerly secured the arm in an air splint. Her mother arrived and transported her to the hospital. You can imagine my surprise when the girl returned to school the next day with casts on BOTH arms.

I enjoy being out on the playground with children. This is referred to in educational circles as "yard duty." It's a real chore for many teachers. This is the time when I can really get to know children personally. No one mandates that principals in the district spend time on the playground. It is my belief that the practice pays dividends. For instance, the lunch break is generally a time when many discipline problems occur—especially during the final minutes before the bell rings. There are two paid yard duty persons available during the lunch break to supervise children. These persons will generally be high school seniors or mothers who want to help out. They receive little or no training on how to solve behavior problems. If I remain in the office "doing a little paper work," referrals of students for misbehavior on the playground will mount up when the bell rings. I have found it is better to be visible on the playground and have the yard supervisors handle the problems they can and send for me if the problem is more than they can handle. In addition, I believe it makes a big difference in the way children behave when they know their principal is on the playground. So this is one of those duties which I have taken on that I really enjoy. I am very bad at remembering and learning names. I make it a point to learn a few new names every day. While I cannot claim that I know the names of all the children at my school, I have heard students comment, "Gosh, he knows everyone's name." Being involved with children and just being around them are the best parts of this job of being a principal to me.

Indeed, principals are involved in the darndest things! It is hard to say that any of the things we do are nonessential. The children who make up my student body today will be the adults who will serve me in restaurants, be my lawyer, doctor, dentist, barber, or what-have-you tomorrow. I want to be able to hold my head up and say that I did everything in my power to help prepare them for the world they will face. I do not wish to be remembered as the mean old principal who constantly meted out punishment and harsh words. I want to be their friend as well as an adult on whom they can depend.

5

WHAT'S IT TO YA?

William Delaney Gibbs attended my school from the fourth through the sixth grades. I had to look back through the school annuals to remember what he looked like. President Bush gave the order in January, 1990, to send additional troops to Panama to capture General Noriega and bring stability to the whole situation in that country. The morning following his decision to send our troops to Panama, I was reading the local newspaper about the predawn invasion when I ran across the name of William Delaney Gibbs, the first American soldier killed in action in Panama. The article stated that Gibbs, who was assigned to the 7th Infantry Division at Fort Ord, California, had been in Panama since October, 1989. He was married in Modesto, California, the previous summer, and his wife was expecting their first child. I learned that Gibbs had attended local schools since the fourth grade, and when the article mentioned the name of my school, I immediately began to try to remember him. When I arrived at school, even before I had a chance to look in the school annuals, the fourth grade teacher to whose class Gibbs had been assigned in 1977 came into my office looking rather forlorn, plopped down in a chair bracing his head in both hands, and sighed deeply. I shared the same feelings he was experiencing.

We knew him as Delaney Gibbs, a tow-headed kid who was every parent's dream. He was well-mannered, excellent in sports, and an overall good student. He got along with everyone. Gibbs' fourth grade teacher stands well over six feet tall, a big man with a beard who speaks with a loud, gruff voice. Students at our school have a healthy respect for him. While he is a firm disciplinarian, he also genuinely cares about children. Over the years I have developed a profound respect for this dedicated teacher who has totally committed himself to youngsters. On this particular morning as he reminisced about Gibbs, he unashamedly shed tears. He had lost one of his own, and it hurt deeply.

Children who attend Stanislaus are like an extension of our own families. We are involved in their lives. When one of the children hurts, we hurt. When we learn of a former student's success in his or her endeavors, we share that success. When a student's life ends tragically, we feel the loss too.

How does a principal and the school cope with death? Whether the issue comes up in a small rural school such as ours or a large city school, staff and students need to be prepared to deal with it. Families, children, and staff may need professional help. Principals can direct them to available counseling services. Other ideas the principal can share include:

1. Provide support for children who experience significant losses. These counseling sessions may be led by teachers, psychologists, counselors, or the principal.

2. Teachers may teach lessons or units on death. They may invite speakers to come to school to talk about death.

3. The parent newsletter may include helpful hints on how to talk to children about death, why it is important

for them to attend the funeral, and how to answer their questions.

4. Parents may inform the school of a death in the family, including a pet. A request to be informed of this information could be included in the student handbook.

5. Provide in-service training for staff on how to handle deaths that occur.

6. Purchase books for the library.

7. Know your own feelings regarding death.

8. Provide some ways to respond. The best things to say are simple and straight forward, such as: "I'm sorry about your friend's death." "I heard about your loss. What can I do to help?" Or, "I don't know what to say."

Sometimes principals are asked to serve on review teams which go into a school to evaluate the school's programs and effectiveness. In our district review teams composed of the curriculum director, an administrator from another school, a school board member, and several teachers from the school being reviewed are assigned the task of conducting these annual, internal reviews. On one occasion when I was serving on a review team for one of the district schools, I went into a primary classroom where students were involved in the study of mathematics. As members of the review team we are encouraged to observe what is happening, walk around the room, interview staff members, and talk with children about their work.

Most of the children were on task, diligently undertaking the problems at hand. One little guy was obviously very frustrated and was madly trying to erase an answer he had decided was incorrect. He had not gone far through the assigned problems, but it was apparent that either his eraser or the paper he was working on would call it a day long before recess. Peering over his shoulder, and in a mood to be helpful, I asked him what he was doing. I was somewhat surprised when he responded, "What's it to ya?"

Children come to our public schools from many and varied backgrounds. We as educators must accept them as they come. Most of us who have been around education for some time know well the saying, "Accept them where they are and take them as far as you can." I wasn't ready to give up with this young man, so I bravely ventured forth to offer my assistance. He was working on subtraction problems which required regrouping. When I suggested that he needed to borrow a "one" from the ten's place, move it to the one's column, and then subtract, his cheeks puffed up and became very red. He exhaled loudly, and what appeared to be smoke came out his ears. I suggested that he have a nice day and quickly departed to observe elsewhere in the classroom. It was clear to me that this young man was going to figure it out all by himself.

Children are a lot of fun. If I were asked to name the single most important reason why I chose education as my life's work, I would have to say without hesitation that it is because I enjoy children. Of course, there are those days when I would deny ever having said that. There are times when problems mount up, reports are due, or other "unmentionable" pressures cloud this vision, but for the most part, children are a joy to be around. They make my day!

I enjoy visiting classrooms. Many times when I walk into a primary classroom I will be greeted by several little persons who come up to show me what they are doing or to hug me. I receive most of these hugs around knee high! I need to make it clear that I do not encourage students to come over to me when I am visiting a classroom. They just do it. However, not too much time goes by before the teacher will have trained the students to be more restrained when visitors (even the principal) come to the room.

Hugs are fun. Everyone should be a "hugger." When I go out each morning to meet the buses as they arrive, some of the students will come up and give me a big hug. These are mostly primary children, and I generally know which ones these will be. It's interesting to observe children's behavior— like their comfort level. Some children want your attention, but they do not want to get too close. Different backgrounds and culture training play a major role in this behavior, I'm sure. For instance, one group, which I call my "Latin Contingent," gets off of the bus and greets me *en masse*. Anywhere from three to six of these little Mexican-American children run up and throw their arms around me (my legs mostly because they are so small). There are three Hindu children who arrive at school each morning and come up to shake my hand. They have seen other children receiving hugs and want to share in their own way of greeting the principal. Children in higher grades react quite differently. Very appropriately, many of these same children who would give me a hug when they were in the primary grades (remember, I've been at this school forever) will share a "high five" in passing. Sometimes when I visit the upper grade classrooms and the mood is just right, one of these students will say, "Give me five, Mr. D." I'm sure my face turns red each time this happens as I feel the eyes of the teacher burn into me for disrupting the class. But, it does give me a warm feeling inside as I hastily make my retreat.

Twice during the school year students with good behavior records are rewarded with a skating party. Teachers are rewarded too because they are not required to supervise their students at the skating rink. Some teachers and many parents of the primary children come along to help with shoe sizes, lacing and tying, and to enjoy skating themselves. At one of the most recent skating parties as students were in line to get their skates, Helen, a little first grade girl, curved her index finger and motioned for me to come over to her.

I thought, "Oh, no! What could be the matter? Was she sick from the bus ride? Had she wet her pants (it happened with another child on that same trip)? Was someone hitting her?" So I hurried over to her and leaned down to hear what she wanted to tell me.

Helen planted a big kiss on my cheek, and whispered (I don't know why she was whispering. Everyone was already watching!), "I sure do love you."

It was time for dramatics. I touched the spot on my cheek where Helen had kissed me and fell over backwards landing on the carpet with a thud. Children know that I joke around a lot. They broke out into uncontrolled laughter.

What's it to me? Just about everything!

6

WHAT'S FOR LUNCH?

The San Joaquin Valley of California is socked in by fog during the winter months, and many parents call to find out if the buses will be running late. But the most frequent call we receive in the office is "What are we having for lunch today?" This is despite the fact that the lunch menus are printed in the local newspaper each week, the office staff sends home a menu to all students each month, and the main courses are listed in the Parent Newsletter which goes home each month. There are as many calls about lunch from parents as there are from children. Perhaps a telephone recording would save us a lot of work. We could follow the example of movie theaters that tell the caller what movies are playing. In her nice, soft-spoken voice, the secretary could pre-record the daily lunch menu. During the foggy season, we could even throw in, "The buses are running two hours late today."

I guess this is as it should be. We are a society that cares a great deal about food and eating. Our students even enjoy a snack recess where everything from tacos to Twinkies is gobbled down at mid-morning in just a few minutes. A few years ago when the country was on a "nutrition kick" the staff decided to regulate the type of snacks children brought to

41

school. We wanted to suggest that parents send carrot or celery sticks, apples, raisins, peanuts, trail mix or any of those "healthy" foods rather than chocolate bars and cupcakes. Unfortunately, this idea never got off the ground.

The cafeteria at Stanislaus School is an interesting place to be. We have the standard rules:

- No running
- No throwing
- No hats
- Clean up your area

But, other than these few rules, coming into the cafeteria is just like eating at one of the local fast food establishments that kids love so much. What could be more fun than sitting with your friends, eating, and talking about the myriads of things kids talk about.

One attempt at moderating the noise level in the cafeteria took shape in a project called QUIET DAY. On this designated day each week a red circle (those familiar with Lee Canter's *Assertive Discipline* procedures will recognize that symbol) was displayed on the door as students entered the cafeteria to let them know that it was "Quiet Day." Tables were numbered, and individuals at the table which was judged the quietest received a free ice cream. Once in awhile we have tried playing music in the cafeteria using a microphone next to a tape recorder. No sophisticated technology here! This produced predictable results. Children talked more loudly. Turn up the music, and they talked louder still. Don't get me wrong, the noise level is not that bad—unless you are super sensitive to noise anyway. Many people have made comments about our cafeteria. The food service manager, who regularly visits all school site cafeterias, said, "I like your way of operating. You let the kids be normal, like real people."

Children are expected to be quiet and work hard in the classrooms. It is unrealistic (and inhumane, in my opinion) to expect them to come into the cafeteria and remain quiet. When we as adults eat together, it would take an act of God for us to eat without talking, or laughing, or having a good time. Our students respect this right which they have earned by their responsible behavior. Children are not marched into the cafeteria and herded onto the next available bench until every seat is filled whether it be by a boy or girl. Boys and girls this age generally do not enjoy sitting together. If they do sit together it is their choice. In our cafeteria children sit where they want within their grade level. Food fights? There has been a skirmish or two in the past few years, but no major battles. The punishment for an offense such as this is to pick up ALL the "stuff" in the cafeteria for a few days. And even a more severe punishment results when the student misses being involved in an intramural game on the playground because he is doing KP.

The student body is like one huge family in the cafeteria at noontime. We have two lunch periods—one for primary and one for intermediate students. Everything that happens at your dinner table—and then some, happens in the cafeteria.

We have spills. Do we ever have spills! I really don't look forward to days when spaghetti or beef gravy (also known by the kids as "barf-a-rony) is served. It is absolutely amazing to watch first graders juggle the components (milk, hot pack, cold pack) of their lunch as they navigate precariously toward their table. When someone spills milk on the floor, I say, "Watch out for the Milky Way!" as children walk by on their way to the table areas until someone comes back with paper towels to clean it up. I get some "Are you crazy?" looks.

We have tears. It seems like a cold, cruel world to a little primary person when he has lost lunch or milk money, when a person sitting nearby calls him names or takes part of his lunch (not the peas and carrots either), or when a retainer inside an unmarked, brown paper bag is dropped into the trash can, the trash cans are full, and besides we're not even sure which trash can was used.

We have fun. A bulletin board in the cafeteria features children who have a birthday that month. Children write their name and birth date with a flair pen on the butcher paper. On the last school day of each month, children who have had a birthday that month are called to the front of the cafeteria where we sing happy birthday to them. They also receive a free ice cream paid for by the Student Council. We give away lots of ice cream. The Student Council members take turns selling ice cream one day each week.

Some parents join their child for a meal in the cafeteria. One father who owns a large restaurant in town eats with his daughter regularly. Sometimes grandparents come to eat with us. A few teachers are even brave enough to eat with their class from time to time.

Primary classes are currently engaged in a "CLEAN" contest to see which class has the cleanest area. Every few weeks, the winning class earns a popcorn party. Who said kids are messy? The cafeteria area could pass a white glove inspection when these little people get through cleaning. They pore over the daily point chart like a stockbroker reading the *Wall Street Journal.*

I have fun teasing children about some of the menu choices. Our food service manager learned a long time ago that children are just not going to eat certain foods. These foods, like carrots, peas, spinach, and corn (all the good veggies), were eliminated from the menu in favor of selections which consistently produced high lunch counts. Some of the main menu items now include corn dogs, Chulupas, pizza, hot dogs, hamburgers, submarine sandwiches, enchiladas, and grilled cheese sandwiches. When grilled cheese sandwiches are served, I pass by a table and comment, "Oh, you're having gorilla cheese today." The kids have that quizzical look on their faces. I let them know the cook and her helpers just returned from a gorilla hunt. The hunting was good, so they could expect gorilla cheese quite often. I also tell them that gorillas have yellow blood and they need to be careful not to get it on anyone. I get the usual "Yuck!" as I continue on my way.

When we sell ice cream, one of the flavors is a lime juice bar. I have fun with this one by calling out, "Anyone want a spinach bar?" This produces lots of "yuck" and "take it away" comments, but amazingly lots of children enjoy this flavor. We offer chocolate milk as a special treat every day. When we run out (it's a popular item!), an intermediate student who did not get to buy chocolate milk will come up to voice his displeasure. My standard comment is, "Sorry, the brown cows were out on strike yesterday." When the cooks prepare spaghetti, sometimes a child will find a parsley leaf in his serving. I say, "Oh, no, I thought we got all those leaves out! The kitchen door was open and some of the leaves the custodian was raking blew into the kitchen." Of course, I quickly explain to the puzzled listeners that I'm kidding, and I give them the proper explanation for the presence of "leaves" in their spaghetti.

This is REALLY a true story. Enough years have passed so that I think I can safely tell it now. Much of the food that is received by schools is frozen. It is stored in a large walk-in freezer until ready for use. The central kitchen is located at my school where food is prepared and distributed via truck to the other school sites in the district. Food is kept hot in zippered warming bags as it travels to these other sites. One day corn dogs were served in the cafeteria. Everyone was enjoying his corn dog. The primary classes had all come through the serving line, sat and eaten their lunch, and gone out to play. The intermediate students were just coming into the cafeteria. A few students had come through the serving line, received their food, and were enjoying it until one creative eater peeled away the crust and exclaimed, "Look at this green wiener!" Upon examination, it turned out that all (or at least a very, very large portion) of the wieners at this table were indeed green. The food service manager immediately called all of the other schools and told them to stop serving the corn dogs. Cold sandwiches were prepared and delivered to the schools. But, all of the primary children at all of the schools had already consumed gobs of green wieners concealed in their corn dogs. Yummm! Fortunately, there were no reports of anyone getting sick, and no irate parents called to complain about the cafeteria serving "green wieners." It is even possible that only a small portion of the wieners were green. No one will ever know.

Many of the products produced today in the food service industry create minor problems for children and major problems for those of us who supervise in school cafeterias. Children can either buy a hot lunch or bring their own lunch from home. It's about half and half. Some of the frustrations we deal with daily involve trying to open the containers. One of the most common problems occurs when the ring on the pudding or fruit cup breaks off. Most of us do not carry a can opener around in our pockets, so we have to come up with creative ways to open the can without severing a finger. Packaged cheese sticks are a real headache too. No one is supposed to carry a knife at school (Basic Rule #121), but it would be difficult for me to survive in the cafeteria without one. Of course, the kids always say, "Shame on you for having a knife." Perhaps the item that is most frustrating to help children with is a packaged drink which has a straw secured to the back. You have to remove the straw and get the protective paper off it (hard for primary children) before inserting the straw into the designated area at the top of the container. What happens, unless you are extremely careful, is that the straw goes through front and back of the container, juice spills on the floor (or me), and the child is in tears because the principal has messed up his drink!

One seemingly quite normal day when the cafeteria was

full of intermediate children, a small, chocolate-colored dachshund came tearing through the cafeteria with the custodian in close pursuit. I told the children not to worry. The custodian would catch the dog before the end of the day, and hot dogs would be served as scheduled the next day. What's for lunch? You never know. It could be "Cook's Surprise!"

7

THERE BE CRITTERS!

I would like to follow up on the story about the dachshund. Stray dogs are a common occurrence around schools. Dogs that appear at this country school, however, are usually runaways or have been let out of cars in the dark of night. The food service manager came to my office holding this small, brown male doxie. His life had been spared. She had not served him as a hot dog.

She said, "How would you like to take him home?"

Of course the secretary, and anyone else standing close by, agreed about how cute he was. He was on his best behavior! Funny, how that works. Everyone knows how much I like dachshunds, so I was the obvious choice to take him if no one came to claim him.

"Let me think it over, and I'll get back to you," I said in typical managerial style.

She agreed to take the doxie home with her overnight. If I didn't want him, we would try to find him a home with one of the children.

When I took Fred (That's want we named him.) home, my children fell in love with him—for a short while at least. That dog was all over everything! Good manners were out the window. He would run from room to room jumping on the beds, bounce into the living room onto the couch, run from one end to the other, hop on the floor and start the routine again. And did he chew! Nothing was safe. He chewed on everything in sight. At night he insisted on sleeping with my daughter. She was a teenager at that time, and everything had to be just so. Fred and my daughter became fast enemies. It wasn't long before Fred became bored with this family. Everyone was gone all day. There were no cats around to chase (Fred loved to chase cats), and there was no one to watch him perform all his cute little tricks. So, Fred decided that the dog food might be better on the other side of town—or wherever—and he left. I still suspect one of my kids purposely let him out and said, "Bye, see you later, dude." Of course, no one at school believed a word of this. They wondered what we did to that "cute, sweet, cuddly" little dog with all the personality.

I have mentioned before that Stanislaus School is surrounded by orchards. Along with the almond orchards, we are blessed with an overabundance of gophers and ground squirrels. One Saturday during the summer a few years before I became principal, rumor had it that over three hundred gophers lost their lives when a flash flood deluged the playground. Farmers in the area flood irrigate their land. One of the farmers agreed to flood the entire playground. I always wondered how they took a body (gopher) count? Anyway, that effort to rid the campus of gophers did not work. We still have many gophers.

Gophers play havoc with a playground. They burrow up and leave huge mounds. When it rains or the field is watered, the mounds collapse leaving holes everywhere. All the usual games are played on our playground. We have boys' and girls' baseball leagues in the spring and summer, soccer in the fall, and our own intramural program during the school year. Efforts are made to keep the holes filled, but it's mostly a losing battle. So far, the gophers have chosen to remain outside. There have been no reports of them appearing in the classrooms.

I can't say the same thing about ants. During certain times of the year we have ant problems. The problem is generally discovered around snack or lunch time when a teacher calls the office to report that ants are devouring lunches which are placed on a shelf until lunch. We have a very small variety of red ants. They don't bite, but they are chocaholics. One year the ants had a field day with candy that was stored in my office for the annual candy sale. The school is fumigated on a regularly scheduled basis to take care of critters like these. Despite the best efforts made, we will probably continue to have our "lunch eating" friends. Their visits provide excellent material for creative writing and art activities.

The critters I have discussed so far have been uninvited. One first grade teacher is noted for the abundance of reptiles in his classroom. The most ominous of these creatures is his seven foot long boa constrictor. The boa has a large, specially built glass cage. There have been tortoises, turtles, lizards, other types of snakes, and fish in his classroom over the years. This year he has added a rather fat, eighteen-inch lizard. A few years ago one afternoon when children had mostly all gone for the day, a rather loud scream resounded from this first grade classroom which is located just across the hallway from the office. The secretary rushed over to see what was happening and came in just in time to see the boa snap up a live rat. The large lump created by the consumed rat was a sight to behold. Several children from this classroom had received parent permission to remain after school and see this demonstration. What a lesson! I know they will never forget it. Neither will the secretary.

Just one more incident about the snake. The summer I was repainting the interior of the classrooms, the boa had not yet left for vacation. He (I don't know; maybe it's a "she") doesn't stay at school during summer months, so I assume he goes on vacation. The boa escaped from his cage and went out of the classroom through the door which opens up on a long hallway. The custodian almost had a heart attack when he arrived at school and discovered that the snake was missing. He evidently wanted to escape the heat and/or the paint smell which pretty well permeated the entire building. All of the outside doors and windows had been secured, so we were sure the boa was somewhere in the building. The teacher was called and an all-points search was conducted for the missing critter. He had escaped before and was always found either in a dark corner or on a sunny cabinet top in the classroom. Once he was found just outside the classroom door in the hallway. The doors were closed and all of the windows except one were locked. The one window that was open is located approximately ten feet up. I still find it hard to believe that the snake slithered up and out that window. This time there was no snake to be found anywhere. He did not come when called, could not be lured out with "live rats," and wasn't even convinced to surrender during the next few weeks when loud, country-western music was blaring down the hallway as we continued painting. The painting task was done, school would begin soon, and the snake was all but forgotten. It was assumed that he had found a way to the outside world and was living happily in the field or orchards devouring rats and gophers to his heart's content. The custodians, however, did walk around warily for awhile. Some of the teachers come back from their summer vacation early to get their rooms set up so that they can enjoy the final days before they must officially report back to work. A kindergarten teacher came back to work in her room. She was in the Supply Room which is located directly at the end of the hallway about two classrooms from the missing snake's winter residence. She was merrily going about the business of gathering supplies when she discovered she was not alone.

I'm not sure if it was her singing or her perfume, but for whatever reason, the boa decided that vacation must be over and it was time to come out of hiding. The rendezvous between Eve and the Serpent in the Garden of Eden and this kindergarten teacher's close encounter had little in common. The kindergarten teacher did not give the snake the time of day. She was out of there! The snake surrendered somewhat peacefully and was returned to his room environment. The kindergarten teacher thought it was a set-up. Who could blame her? I think that was the year she retired.

One year was particularly wet with more than the average amount of rainfall. This seemed to entice many field mice to come inside the main building where the staff lounge was located at that time. The mice were escaping the cold, wet winter and also searching for food. They found plenty of food literally at both ends of the building. The building is anchored at one end by two kindergarten rooms which are notorious for their abundance of snack foods such as graham crackers and at the other end by the staff lounge which also has a well earned reputation for being cluttered. Staff persons are assigned on a rotation basis to clean the lounge, but the mice didn't need to search all that hard to find things to eat. These little fellows were hard to catch. We had to take extra care because of the children. This is the case when trying to exterminate gophers, spiders, mosquitoes, flies, mice, or any other unwelcome pests around a school. We did succeed in getting rid of the mice.

I need a full-time custodian just to keep the school free from spider webs. Being in the country, we are blessed with an abundance of spiders. Some aren't the friendly type. Several black widows have been found on the premises. The spider web problem is a constant frustration for all of us. The secretaries have their own unique system of calling the custodian's attention to spider webs. When a web has existed without being removed for a few days, they call the custodian's attention to it by writing a note with an arrow pointing to the web. The note is taped to the wall, ceiling, or window so that it cannot be missed when the room is being cleaned. Amazingly the spider web is gone the next day—occasionally even some dust along with it.

Bees occupy our attention every spring. When the blossoms appear on the almond trees, the bees are turned loose to do their work. We always put out a "Bee Alert" to inform teachers to discuss procedures when playing around the bees. In the office we pay special attention to registration cards where parents have indicated that their child is allergic to bee stings. The bees are really quite harmless—unless they are provoked; i.e., children batting them away will provoke them.

The most current unwanted guests at our school were a family of skunks. I can smell a skunk a mile away, and I thought I was dreaming when I came to school one morning in August before teachers or students had arrived and smelled that telltale odor. I quickly found the custodian and asked him to tell me that it wasn't true. There simply are not skunks in this area. I grew up in central Texas where there are as many skunks as we have gophers, so I was well aware of problems we could encounter if these critters had taken up residence with us. The custodian told me that he suspected the skunks had found a home under one of the relocatable classrooms. Several means to persuade the varmints to leave failed, and in fact, school was back in session before the problem was solved. Can you imagine being in a sixth grade classroom with a family of skunks underneath? But then again, sixth grade children are entering that time of life when they could give skunks a run for the money.

I went out to school very late one night. The night custodian had already gone home. I decided to enter the building through the kindergarten room at the farthest end from the office area. The light switch in this room is located on the opposite wall, so I had to feel my way across the room in the dark. My eyes had not become accustomed to the dark as I was slowly making my way across the room. You can imagine my surprise when a white blur whizzed past me. I just about jumped out of my skin. I'm sure the rabbit had the same idea, and he was much more adept at jumping (or was it hopping?). I hurriedly reached the opposite side of the room, felt around for the light switch, switched on the light, and turned around to face Brer Rabbit. I know my limits and I'm not exactly the fastest one in a foot race. I figured my chances of catching that rabbit would be just about as productive as discussing kindergarten curriculum with him, so I hastily turned off the light and exited through the closest door.

8

THE PRINCIPAL'S OFFICE

There are two ways of looking at "The Principal's Office." The first is the actual physical place where the principal works on the school premises. The second is the office of the principal, or in other words, his "role" at the school.

A sign on my secretary's desk states:

> *Do you want to talk to the boss, or to the person who really knows what's going on?*

There is probably a great deal of truth in that. Charlotte, my secretary, is a wonderful person. She has served as the secretary at Stanislaus for many years. She is efficient, dependable, and an excellent PR (public relations) person. She's all right except when she sings to my plants. When she sings to the plants for some strange reason, they die. When people come to Stanislaus School, they enter a hallway through the large, double doors of the first building. The first door on the right features a sign which lets the visitor know that he has found the OFFICE.

Visitors often ask the secretary, "Are you the principal?"

She cheerfully replies, "Who wants to know?" or, "Do you have good news or bad news?"

One time I was visiting in a sixth grade classroom during a health lesson. Teachers generally select a student to answer the telephone so that they do not have to stop teaching. While I was sitting in the back of the room, the phone rang and a boy who happened to be President of the Student Council that semester answered it. Class went on as usual while he conversed with the secretary. The conversation ended with him saying, "I love you too." All heads in the room turned in his direction as he headed for his desk. He looked at the teacher, who was also staring at him, and said, matter-of-factly: "Well, she told me she loved me. What could I say?"

The secretary or office staff deals with or wards off salespersons, fund raisers, district office personnel, parents, grandparents, children, teachers, custodians, bus drivers, cafeteria managers, maintenance persons, state inspectors, architects, real estate agents, day care workers, professors, former students, retired teachers, student teachers, librarians, curriculum directors, fire marshals, police officers, sheriff's deputies, PTA presidents, scout leaders, baseball and soccer coaches, 4-H Club leaders, child protective agency workers, psychologists, nurses, people with car trouble, neighbors with domestic problems, insurance adjusters, car salesmen, truck drivers, pest (not children) controllers, risk managers, review teams, auditors, business managers, trash collectors, water purifiers, mosquito abatement teams, newspaper reporters, mailpersons, delivery services, and my own children. No wonder the principal's office is often well-hidden and the principal keeps the door shut!

A door separates my office from the secretary. That door is generally always open. (I'm afraid I will miss something! My secretary knows more gossip than Ann Landers.) There are, of course, many exceptions when the door is shut. When the superintendent comes to call, you can bet we meet behind closed doors. High level discussions going on. Top secret! I still haven't figured out why many people in this business are

so secretive! Besides, this is the best way to start rumors—
"What kind of trouble is the principal in now?"

My staff knows that my door is always open. If a teacher
comes to see me and wants to talk in private, he will initiate
the privacy by closing the door when he comes into the
office. Some, but by no means all, discipline cases are
handled in private. And, parents often feel more comfortable
when they meet with the principal behind closed doors.

One principal I know has an OPEN SCHOOL. There are
very few walls. Areas are divided by bookcases, filing
cabinets, or partitions. This principal has chosen to be right
out in the open. The principal needs to be seen, but I think
that arrangement allows for too much visibility. As a vice
principal I occupied a very small office. There was hardly
room to turn around. It was impossible for me to see more
than two visitors (generally students with behavior problems) at a time with the furniture (desk, chair, and filing
cabinet) in the room. Once a teacher sent nine students to
see me at one time. There was no way we would all fit! We
would have made the *Guinness Book of World Records* if all
of us had squeezed into that room. If the problem was so big
that the teacher had to send me one-third of the class, I
figured we might as well march back to the classroom and
discuss the situation with everyone.

I went from that school with a tiny office to a school where
the principal's office was the largest in the district. The large
desk that belonged to the superintendent who hired me as a
teacher many years before occupied a central position in the
room. Through the large windows which looked out on the
front of the school, I could see a rose garden (roses are my
favorite flower—they are beautiful and they smell nice, but
they also have thorns. Is that an omen?), a nice green stretch
of grass, and the STATE highway which runs east and west and
connects to two other major highways. The office was nicely
paneled and spacious enough to include a round conference

table, two filing cabinets, and bookcases. I was in awe! The floor was carpeted, and all the furnishings matched well enough so that at least it appeared that the things had not come from Good Will Industries. I had arrived!

This was my first job as a principal. What I didn't know would fill volumes. Frankly, it was my impression from principals I have known that the person who filled this role stayed in the office and "did all the paper work." I also figured that the reason the former principal had the huge desk was because of the massive amounts of paper work he was required to complete. I had visited the school only a few times before I became principal. Once the secretary was showing me around, and she led me to the principal's office. She explained that I should not be alarmed by the "desk area." I could not imagine what she meant until I came into the office and saw a large piece of white butcher paper covering the entire length of the desk. There was a sign written with a red flair pen across the steeply-mounded paper that exclaimed:

"PLEASE DO NOT DISTURB THIS MESS.
IT IS ORGANIZED, AND I WILL
GET BACK TO IT LATER!"

Further, I astutely noted that he had positioned the desk in a corner of the office where he would not be exposed to the public, or to anyone else. I wondered about this because I knew him as a "people" person who greatly enjoyed talking with others and being visible. I learned that he and I were similar in one respect. He, too, was a furniture mover. He enjoyed changing the location of his desk. I found myself doing the same thing for a few years until we became computerized, mechanized, and technologized. I would move my desk over by the windows so I could see all the big semi-trucks go by at 70 miles per hour in a 25 mph school zone, watch the rain hit the windows on a cold winter day, or see the teachers leave for the day long before I could. Now the location of my desk has stabilized. It is directly in the center of the room facing the secretary's office and visible to everyone.

What kind of person makes a good principal? My image of this person is quite different from that of many of my colleagues. I'm aware that the principal is supposed to be the chief person, the leader—the head "honcho" of the school. I have no argument with those definitions of the role. There is no question but that I am the leader of my school. However, there are different ways to lead. School principals are no different from leaders in other fields in that their own individual style of leadership is expressed as dictatorial, permissive, decisive, wishy-washy, bossy or benevolent.

What memories I have of principals during my own school years! Were any of them "my hero"? No! Did I want to grow up and become a principal because of their example? No! Did I or could I ever conceive of one of these persons as a friend? No! Would I go back, if I could, and tell any of these principals "thank you" for being a positive influence in my life? No! No! No! Principals of schools I attended were definitely the authoritarian, dictator type.

I was involved in one fight during my elementary school years. My family lived near a military base in government housing during World War II. Children were bused to schools in the nearby town. Our housing complex had one large, very mean bully who beat up on everyone who got in his way. At least that's the way it seemed to me as a skinny little, four-eyed, third grade runt. My sister and this bully were in the same fifth grade class. At the bus stop one morning the two of them became involved in an argument. The bully started fighting my sister. She was definitely getting the worst of it, and what red-blooded little brother is going to stand by and see his sister (with whom he fought all the time himself) get beaten up? So, I attacked—glasses and all. Just a few bruises, a bloody lip, broken glasses, torn pants, and a banana-from-my-lunch-stuffed-in-my-mouth later, the fight was broken up. I think I lost! As I remember it, we all had to visit the principal's office.

I've often wondered since becoming a principal how I come across to children. My childhood principal seemed to have no compassion, was in no mood to listen, and could see no reason for fighting. He definitely would not tolerate fighting at his school. We were all sent home with our parents. Fighting is wrong! I was wrong! But, I would still do it again under the same circumstances. Children are going to have disagreements, and they are going to settle their differences the only way they know how. We as adults can teach them better ways to resolve problems. We can counsel them to think about consequences before they act. Children act the way they do for a reason. I will never be able to understand all the reasons. Life is complex. But, I better be ready, and take the time, to listen. Listen and understand, and in so doing, cause the little people under my charge to feel that they are being treated fairly.

My junior high and high school years were spent in a small central Texas town with a heavy German ancestry. Our junior/senior high school was on the same campus. When I entered the seventh grade, my sister was a freshman. The same principal was overseer of the six hundred students comprising both the junior and senior high areas. The principal, who had been there for many years, was a robust, red-faced Dutchman who was known for his "no nonsense" approach to education.

Assemblies were held in the gym and both junior high and senior high students attended. At the first assembly of the school year, my friends (after this incident nobody would ever claim they knew me!) and I were sitting high up in the bleachers in the gym, when someone in the group (it really wasn't me!) started popping us with his handkerchief (boys don't even carry those any more). Looked like fun to me! Well, the principal saw ME—no one else, just me. He rose from his chair, walked across the gym floor, pointed his finger at me, and shouted, "You! Get down here this minute!"

"Who, me?" I indicated by pointing my index finger at my chest. He turned even redder in the face and yelled, "Right now, sonny." I don't remember wetting my pants at the time, but I almost do now every time I think about that incident.

The principal literally took me by my right ear and pulled me to the center of the gymnasium floor. He declared to everyone in the assembly that "this" young man would stand there for the duration as an example to those who might consider misbehaving during an assembly. My sister never forgave me. My girl friend told me to get lost. My "friends," who were also popping the handkerchiefs, told me how sorry they were, but they stayed miles away for a long, long time. After all, I was a trouble maker and a "real" behavior problem. And, the stock market dropped ten points that day!

I was humiliated and felt that I was unfairly treated. This man was my principal all the way through high school, and he never said a word to me. Eighty-eight students were in my graduating class, and there were fewer than four hundred in the entire high school. I was not a trouble maker. I was a hard worker, and I made good grades. I was never sent to the principal's office. Was it his decisive action at that assembly that molded and shaped me into the fine, upstanding young man who graduated from that high school six years later? I doubt it! But, I can tell you one thing: I will never humiliate one of my students, and, as large as my school may become, I will always make an attempt to learn children's names and to treat them with respect.

Now one for the other side. The Dean of the Department of Religion at Baylor University once gave me some advice which I have remembered and tried to practice. This dean was like a principal in that he was in charge of student discipline. I had a double major, religion and English, and was doing quite well in both subject areas. I was taking a tough class on the history and development of the Baptist Church from a professor who had a reputation for being stingy with grades. His usual practice was to give one "A" in each class. I had studied hard for the exam, but as I was going through the questions, I knew my preparation was not adequate and my answers were rambling. I finished the test. We were required to write "The oath" at the end of our work and sign our name to it.

The oath stated, "I have neither given nor received help on this test nor have I seen others do so."

I dutifully wrote the oath and signed it. Then, I added a "PS." Big mistake! The "PS" was short, but written in large print. It exclaimed, "PHOOEY!"

The next day the professor announced to the class that the Dean wanted to see me. Wow! The DEAN wanted to see me. I didn't even know what a "dean" was! When I arrived at his office, he politely invited me to sit down. I know it must have been difficult for him to contain himself. I have had discipline cases that were so funny, I was hard pressed to keep from laughing out loud. And this was funny! I'm sure he had never dealt with such an incorrigible student! In a very calm, almost subdued voice, he asked me if I would mind explaining the word I had written on my exam. He convinced me that my attitude was not appropriate for a religion major and warned me that if I didn't repent I would be expelled from the college. He listened patiently as I told my story about how I was struggling financially just to remain in school, working forty hours a week, and taking a full load of classes. Then he took his Bible and turned to Proverbs 24:10, which says:

"If you falter in times of trouble, how small is your strength?" Next he turned to Proverbs 16:3, pushed the Bible across the desk toward me and told me to read it.

"Commit to the Lord whatever you do, and your plans will

succeed." He took time, as insignificant as this problem was, to listen to me and give me some good advice.

I probably stand way out on a limb with my personal philosophy of what a principal should be, but it makes sense to me, and so far I haven't been fired or shot. To me the principal is a servant. First, I feel like my primary role is to "be there" for teachers. Second, I think it is my job to serve the children who attend my school. I view the school as a large family. The teachers are like the wife, and the students are the children. If I as a principal can keep my teachers happy, we together will do a much better job of meeting the children's needs.

I made up my mind a long time ago that no matter what happened, I needed to be myself. I followed a very successful, dynamic principal at the school I serve now. I could not be him. I could not come close to measuring up to his accomplishments. He was personality plus. I was quiet and reserved. He was an extrovert. I am an introvert. He had years of experience. I was just beginning. On his evaluations I'm sure he must have received "EXCELLENT" ratings. I knew I would always be just "ABOVE THE LEVEL OF SATISFAC- TORY." I had learned some things as a vice principal about how not to do things when I became a principal. I definitely did not want to paddle children (that was when principals could paddle). I would not demean or ridicule children or staff. I would not run away from, cover up, or avoid problems. I wanted teachers to be responsible for classroom behavior problems. I did not want to be the "Heavy." I would support teachers even when they were wrong, but at the same time, do all I could to help them improve. I would listen, listen, listen!

9

TAKE A NUMBER

Teachers gave me a mug (a more popular gift than a tie these days) for Bosses' Day one year. The saying on the mug reads:

Take a number. Now serving:
4,738

The principal's time is much in demand. One of the greatest demands, if not THE greatest, on his time is student discipline. The first year I served as a vice principal, there were days when I couldn't come up for air. A seemingly endless stream of students flowed through my office. I was so busy "putting out fires" that I had no time to analyze the situation to try to discover why or how the fires were being started in the first place. I was transferred to the district's largest elementary school from the junior high to gain administrative experience at that level. During my tenure there the school had some classes on double sessions. You know what that means! We had double the number of students the school had been built to house and half the help we needed to do an effective job. This was a real proving ground for me.

That first year 1,077 students were referred to my office

with behavior problems. Many of these were, of course, repeaters—students who were sent to the office more than once. The principal, my boss, let it be known that he would take care of all teacher observations and evaluations. My job was discipline. I was "The Hammer." And the flood gates were opened! Teachers, custodians, yard duty supervisors, nurses, the principal, neighbors, the policeman in charge of Safety Patrol, the psychologist, and children's parents all contributed to my job security.

The paddle, commonly known as the ferrule in early school days, was the primary means of "correction" used to solve discipline problems at the school. That year the paddle was used 125 times. (Nope, not all my doing. Remember, I came to the school well into the second semester.) When I did choose to paddle a child, even though written parent permission was on file, I called home to let the parent know what was happening. During the next two years, I used the paddle twelve times. I'm not proud of that record. If I had exercised more patience and been more effective as a counselor, I would not have had to use the paddle. The paddle was seldom (and then mostly at parents' request) used during those first few years when it was still "legal" to paddle children at school in California.

The number of children referred to me the last year was just over four hundred. There were that many "repeaters" alone the first year I was there. I learned some valuable lessons from that experience. The staff will gladly send you all of their problems. That's what a vice principal is for, right? But, the staff will also conform to the standards and expectations you set. They will work with you. After all, they want children to behave so they as teachers can be more effective in the classroom. Children, in general, do not set out to be disruptive, defiant, belligerent brats.

A plaque on the wall in my office at home states: "Children learn what they live." If they live with hostility, they will be hostile. If they live with fairness, they will learn justice. It took quite a while for me to learn, but I did learn. In the beginning, I wasn't a very good listener. I just wanted to "solve the problem" and get on to the next one. As a result, I contributed to my own problem by not being thorough.

There had to be some humor in the job, or I never would have survived. I developed a "Verbal Expression Test" based on some of the situations with which I dealt. The test is included later in this chapter. In order to give you a better opportunity to do well on the test, I will prepare you for it by discussing some of the discipline cases. Pay particular attention to expressions which may be foreign to you. They definitely had meaning to the students who used them!

One of the broad categories of discipline cases that principals deal with is name-calling. Children have all kinds of endearing expressions to "lay on one another." Sometimes the name-calling is directed at adults. One of the parents who had been hired to help supervise children was working in the cafeteria. I was able to determine from conversations shared with me by students who had been referred that this person was very strict. It was all I could do to maintain my composure when a boy sitting across from my desk shared with me the reason why he was referred to my office. The referral form did, in fact, state that the reason for the referral was that he called the supervisor a name. The name was not included on the referral. The young man was quite hesitant to repeat what he had called her. After some coaxing, plea bargaining, and maneuvering, he admitted to calling her a "bubble gum butt," but he quickly added that he was not the author of the expression. He told me that this endearing expression was commonly used by most of his peers in reference to this cafeteria supervisor.

Another type of name-calling involves the use of vulgar language directed at friends and enemies alike. These words (commonly referred to as four-letter words) are often cloaked in "sound alike" terms that children make up to "cover their tracks." Two of these expressions which I have dealt with repeatedly are "the F-word" and "As so." A second grade boy was referred by a yard duty supervisor at noon for calling another boy the "F-word." I received the citation from the secretary, and directed the young man to a chair in my office. I asked him if he knew why he had been sent to the office. He said he didn't know. He couldn't think of a single thing he had done wrong, but he had a woeful tale about many others who were doing wrong to him. I read him the message on the referral form.

"Did you call the boy the F-word," I asked.

"Well, yes, but he was calling me names too," he replied.

"Can you tell me what the "F" stands for in the word that you called him?

I almost fell out of my chair when he replied with a straight face, "It means fart face."

A boy and a girl in the sixth grade had been good friends, but a rift developed between them. They were engaged in an argument, a real shouting match, when a teacher intervened and sent them to the office. Each admitted to calling the other names, but the boy insisted that he had not called the girl an "ass hole" (the term used on the office referral form by the teacher). I asked him what he did call her, if not that.

Without even hesitating and with a straight face, he replied, "I said she was just 'as so'."

"And what did you mean by that?" I asked as I tried to conceal the smile that was trying to creep across my face. I quickly put my hand up to my chin to help conceal this terrible weakness I felt developing!

"Well, I don't think she is THAT good-looking. She's just 'as so'," he said.

"I think you have your words confused. Don't you mean that she is just 'so-so'?"

There wasn't enough evidence to convict, but I highly

suspect he knew what he was talking about—in both instances.

Children today are bombarded by bad language in movies, on television, in magazines, and in newspapers. They hear it from older children, adults, and from their peers. It's no wonder then that children often use bad language to express how they feel. If we agree as educators that bad language has no place in the classroom or on the playground, we must constantly wage the battle to stop its use.

Many times children do not want to repeat the bad language they used which resulted in their meeting with the vice principal. One tactic I encountered on occasion was the expression, "bleep," as used by the media to blot out an unacceptable word. Once I asked a student to tell me what he said, and he replied that he had told his friend to "Go to BLEEP!"

A referral form I received from a third grade teacher stated that the boy named on the form had used "fowl *(sic)* language" directed toward a young lady in the class. She would like me to severely reprimand him. When you are sitting there reading the form the student has handed you and you have seen more than your quota of behavior problems during the day, it is hard to keep from cracking up when a funny one comes along. The teacher obviously meant "foul" language, but I wondered if she were comparing the boy's response to the low, guttural utterances drakes make when trying to attract the opposite sex. No, probably not, but I had a good laugh later when I shared the spelling mistake with the teacher.

There are myriads of referrals dealing with restroom situations. For some reason unknown to me (it wasn't covered in my master's program), children seem to believe that the fixtures in the restroom are there for the purpose of body development. They use the bar above the partitions as a chinning device, they climb on the toilets and sinks and jump down, and they develop their curve ball by wetting paper towels and throwing them at each other and the walls. The restroom is also an excellent place to entertain friends, play tag, to run to in order to escape when being chased, and to play ball.

The funniest restroom case I recall involved an eight-inch, red, rubber playground ball and a first grade boy. The boy was referred by his teacher when he returned to the classroom from recess, and other boys "finked" on him. The referral from the teacher stated, "Jack peed on this ball." That's how I got it! The referral form was scotch taped to the ball! This was in the days before we were encouraged to wear plastic gloves in dealing with various and sundry situations at school. So, I delicately sat the ball with attached referral form on the floor and began the interrogation.

"Did you, in fact, go to the bathroom (he would not have understood had I asked him if he urinated) on the ball?"

With head down, "Yes, but I was mad."

"Why were you so angry at the ball?" I asked.

"These boys were throwing the ball around in the bathroom. I was trying to go to the bathroom, but they wouldn't let me by."

He hesitated, and I had to encourage him to continue his story.

"When they wouldn't let me by, I just got real mad so I . . . ," he said as his head dropped another few inches toward his chest. He wasn't able to finish the sentence, and I didn't make him.

I'm sure you get the rest of the picture. I wanted to ask him if it was a moving or still shot . . . but I didn't.

The Verbal Expression Test referred to earlier in this chapter has been field tested by two faculties. I administered the test during a faculty meeting at the school where I served as vice principal, it produced many chuckles and outright laughter which may have skewed the results. When I gave the test at my present school, some of the flavor was lost. This staff had not been through the experience (WAR?). We did not have the sheer volume of behavior problems with which to deal. I gave the test to them as an "ice breaker" at the beginning of the meeting. They thought it was REAL until they got into it. Looking at the test now, some fifteen years later, it is amazing to me how language changes. Children today don't use the word "nerd," and whoever heard of a "Woosie?" It's time for a test revision to align the behavior language!

Here's the original test:

VERBAL EXPRESSION TEST FROM VICE PRINCIPAL'S LOG

1. accident

   a. low guttural utterances approximating the drake sexual response used by third grade boy to attract a girl's attention

2. bubble gum butt

   b. expressive expletive for a four-letter word meaning "fart face"

3. "F" word

   c. a circular object upon which to urinate in the lavatory in order to vent frustration after being struck by said object

4. go to "BLEEP"

   d. an object to stand upon for the purpose of entertaining peers; indoor physical education equipment

5. "as so"

   e. endearing expression referring to the posterior used to attract the cafeteria supervisor's attention

6. vulgar sign

   f. an affectionate expression used by a boy to tell a sixth grade girl that her figure was okay, but not great

7. fowl language

   g. physical contact between two or more angry participants entered into because one called the other a Woosie

8. ball   h. movement of an appendage to forcefully strike another person

9. nerd   i. teacher's expression describing a boy's culminating activities prior to his exit from the classroom

10. toilet   j. person of either sex who has gained special recognition in the eyes of his/her peers

11. horsing around   k. the raised medial phalanges of the metacarpal which means "Hi" unless pointing straight up at which time it becomes an obscene gesture

12. hassle   l. free advice given to direct a friend with whom there has been a difference of opinion to a specific destination

(*Answers:* h, e, b, l, f, k, a, c, j, d, i, g)

We make rules to cover every situation. A chart titled **PUNISHMENTS** dated November 10, 1848, hangs on my office wall. This chart lists twenty-four rules and the consequences for not obeying these rules. Beside each rule the number of "Lashes" an offender would receive is listed. How times change! The most severe punishment (10 lashes) was reserved for "playing cards at school" and "for misbehaving to girls." The least severe punishments (2 lashes) were delivered to children who came to school with dirty face and hands, wetting each other at playtime (What? Playground balls not included?) and waring *(sic)* long fingernails. The chart, including all the misspelled words, appears as follows:

Lashes

1. Boys and girls Playing Together 4
2. Fighting at School 5
3. Quareling at School 5
4. Gambleing or Betting at School 4
5. Playing at Cards at School 10

Lashes

6. Climbing for Every Foot Over Three Feet Up a Tree 1
7. Telling Lyes 7
8. Telling Tales Out of School 8
9. Giving Each Other Ill Names 3
10. Swaring at School..8
11. For Misbehaving to Girls 10
12. For Drinking Spiritous Liquors at School 8
13. Making Swings and Swinging on Them 7
14. For Waring Long Finger Nails 2
15. Misbehaving to Persons on the Road 4
16. For Going to Girls Play Places............................3
17. For Going to Boys Play Places............................3
18. Coming to School With Dirty Faces and Hands................2
19. For Calling Each Other Liars 4
20. For Wrestling at School 4
21. For Weting Each Other Washing at Playtime 2
22. Scuffling at School 4
23. For Going and Playing about the Mill or Creek................6
24. For Going about the Barn or doing any Mischief
    about the Place..7

Rules are important. Children will be more successful in life if they learn to remain within defined limits. An all-inclusive list of rules will never be possible nor is it necessary. Fortunately, in education there has been a movement away from long lists of "do's and don't's" for children to follow in favor of statements which help children become responsible for their own behavior. I like the statement many teachers have framed in their classroom which states:

> "Do not do anything which will take away from my right to teach and the right of others to learn."

If I were to come up with a list of offenses and punishments similar to the one published in 1848, it might look something like the following: (I'll use twenty-four because there must be a good reason why that number was used.)

1. Fighting at school, on the bus, or on the way home
2. Using profanity (including obscene gestures)
3. Being disrespectful to adults
4. For not minding
5. For using or possessing cigarettes, alcohol, or drugs
6. Stealing
7. Lying
8. For kissing girls at recess (popular first grade activity)
9. For squirting others with a water gun
10. For cutting girls' hair with scissors
11. For spitting from the slide
12. For jumping from the swings
13. For chasing girls (or boys)
14. For playing tag on the Tower
15. For running after a ball in the street
16. For pulling a chair out from under another
17. For wrestling or playing rough
18. For writing on walls
19. For chewing gum (or eating candy)
20. For biting other children
21. For popping bags in the cafeteria
22. For throwing rocks, grass, food, or other things
23. For playing in the water
24. For doing mischief about the place (There has to be a catch-all phrase.)

Punishments (listed as Lashes) were outlined for each offense on the 1848 chart. However, working with children (and parents) today requires the principal to take a much different approach. The principal can no longer paddle (lash) children. My one-inch thick, round paddle with a ten-inch diameter still hangs on the wall in the supply closet in my office . . . out of sight and out of mind. Because of all the working parents, it is difficult to reach parents during the school day which, in many cases, makes a suspension away from school impossible. Besides, suspending a child plays into his hands many times because he wants to go home. He can watch television or play all day. Children who receive special education services must be treated differently too. The principal must consult with his team of professionals to decide what action to take. So, in this day of collective bargaining and labor unions, we principals must learn to be effective negotiators in order to come to a consensus about the proper punishment a child should receive.

Children will be children whether it's 1848 or 1990. Consider some of the behaviors of children in the nursery rhymes we all read and enjoy. I've often wondered about "the REST of the story" (as the radio commentator Paul Harvey says) when reading some of these rhymes.

> *"Little Jack Horner*
> *Sat in the corner"*

Why was he sitting in the corner? The verse ends with him saying, "What a good boy am I!" Was he rationalizing when, in fact, he had been placed in the corner because of misconduct? Where did he get the pie? Did he steal it? If you notice, he was eating it without a fork.

Then Jack and Jill had their problems too. Did Jack have ulterior motives in taking Jill up the hill? Did Jill push Jack and cause him to fall down the hill because he was getting "too fresh?" Next, he probably grabbed her arm as he was falling thus causing her to take a tumble. Notice though what happens when Jill gets home and laughs. She's the one who got the spanking! Sure she laughed, but so did Jack. Was favoritism being shown here? Anyway, it all ended happily as they go off together to play on the seesaw.

So many of the nursery rhymes include a character named "Jack." I counted fourteen rhymes in a short period of time that gave Jack top billing. I would avoid that name if I were a young parent considering names for children today. Consider:

"Jack be nimble,
Jack be quick,
Jack jump over
the candle stick."

Is this the same Jack who had a friend named Jill? It seems from the verse that he might be a hyperactive child. Was he playing with fire? If this is the same Jack who is spoken of in the verse,

"When Jacky's a good boy,
He shall have cakes and custard;
But when he does nothing but cry,
He shall have nothing but mustard."

It's no wonder that he has problems. His parents (or is it the school's responsibility?) need to take a good look at his diet. If he is getting into a lot of mischief at school, the district might even spring for a complete medical examination! He definitely needs to be referred to the Child Study Team.

There have been a few "Jack's" at my school. Of course, they went by other names, but the behavior was similar. The most famous Jack at Stanislaus School was an extremely bright young man. When he was in the first grade, his teacher encouraged him to choose a partner and study all aspects of the heart. These two boys prepared their research and, using a plastic, scale model of the heart, presented an outstanding report to the class. Along with his talent, however, this Jack also had a very bad temper. One time he became angry at the teacher as they were working together.

The teacher said, "You're so mad, you would like to hit me, wouldn't you?"

Jack replied, "Yes, in fact I would very much like to hit you."

The teacher told him, "Go ahead, if it will make you feel better."

So Jack slapped the teacher across the face knocking his glasses off. The teacher was totally shocked, but kept his cool. After all, he had invited the boy to hit him.

This same Jack had a habit of biting other children whenever he felt as if there was no other way to defend himself. This behavior continued through the fifth grade.

One day Jack was sent to my office for counseling. He was in the third grade at the time but working with an advanced reading group in another classroom. Jack and I had some interesting conversations all through his elementary school years. He communicated on an adult level, expressed ideas and solutions freely, and didn't hesitate to let me know exactly how he felt. We were discussing his reading placement. The reading text was not too difficult, but he objected to the "busy work" demanded of him in completing the reading workbook. A typical response from Jack would go something like this:

"Now, Lamar . . ." (at which point I would remind him to call me Mr. Dodson), ". . . the way I see it, I shouldn't be required to do the assignments in the reading workbook."

"But, all of the other students in your class must complete those assignments. Sometimes we have to do things we don't especially enjoy, Jack."

"Well, would you just consider letting me use the computer to complete the work using the word processor?" asked Jack.

I lost that battle. Jack eventually returned to his regular classroom and worked independently on his reading assignments.

How about Mary in the rhyme "Mary, Mary quite contrary?" A "contrary" person is one who argues with everyone, according to my dictionary. And if this was the very same Mary who brought her lamb to school when she knew it was against the rules, the picture becomes clearer still. It probably wasn't the first time she brought the lamb either. Sounds to me like Mary might have been the teacher's pet. Mary got away with bringing the lamb to school. She wasn't given lashes in a day and time when it was permissible for the teacher to paddle children in the classroom—without a witness!

Most principals will probably agree that girls do not get into as much mischief as boys. I came close, but I never paddled a girl at school. They're so cute and so sweet, as a rhyme called THE LITTLE GIRL shows:

"There was a little girl, and she had a little curl
Right in the middle of her forehead;
When she was good she was very, very good,
But when she was bad she was horrid."

We have our stereotypes of what boys and girls are like. The most famous rhyme which everyone is familiar with is one called BOYS AND GIRLS:

"What are little boys made of, made of?
What are little boys made of?
Frogs and snails
And puppy-dogs' tails,
That's what little boys are made of.
What are little girls made of, made of?
What are little girls made of?
Sugar and spice
And all things nice,
That's what little girls are made of."

My most famous "Mary," a fifth grader, was very contrary. Mary had a "grade averager" in her possession with a man's name on it. Her teacher took it away because she thought it was hers. The girl told her mother that she was being accused of stealing. Mother, teacher, and Mary had a conference. Mary argued that the "grade averager" was a gift from her former teacher. This teacher was called and verified that he did have a grade averager but that it was missing. He did not know what had happened to it. Grade averagers are not an item a student could easily come by since they must be special ordered. A teacher would certainly not give one to a student. Draw your own conclusions!

Later on, Mary and three other girls were involved in a pushing match. Mary said that she was kicked and that the other girls hurt her back. I investigated the incident, which seemed to be minor in comparison to most discipline referrals I was receiving. I dismissed the girls after counseling and warning them about rough play. A dispute over this incident erupted which lasted for six months. Mary and her mother brought a sheriff's deputy to school with a warrant two months later to reopen the "pushing/kicking" incident. This was after Mary had transferred to another school. The case eventually went to juvenile court, and two of the girls who were accused of kicking Mary were placed on probation for one year. I had known these two girls since kindergarten. They fit the nursery rhyme to a tee . . ."they were very, very good." Neither girl had ever had problems at school. They were model citizens. Mary, on the other hand and as it turns out, had an interdistrict agreement to attend Stanislaus School because she was having so many problems adjusting at another district school. She had only been at that school for a short time. Prior to that she had attended fourth grade across town where she and her mother were infamous. Mary certainly wasn't made of "sugar and spice and everything nice." I have only touched the surface here of a girl with many, many problems. She will forever occupy the number one spot on my list of difficult children with whom I have worked. "When they are bad, they are horrid!"

10

YOUR NUMBER IS UP!

It is difficult to be an effective counselor and be the disciplinarian or authority figure at the same time. These two roles deserve separate hats. Unfortunately, the public is not ready to pay for counseling services at the elementary level. When I was a vice principal, I saw multitudes of children with problems. They were constantly in trouble because of their behavior, both in the classroom and on the playground. For the most part I saw repeaters, students who were sent to the office over and over again. In many cases, even the parents could not control them and did not know what to do with them at home. They needed a counselor, not a paddle. I was frustrated because of the volume of referrals coming in and my lack of training to cope with the task. From that experience I learned techniques which I began to implement when I became a principal.

Many teachers seem to have been taught that children MUST be sent to the office for just about everything. Children are going to have disagreements, just as adults do. If we do not give them an opportunity to talk about their differences of opinion and provide them with ways to work out problems cooperatively, we will continue to provide society with problems. When a potential fight appears imminent, I encourage my teachers and yard duty supervisors to allow children to talk to each other and work out their differences. Most of the time, I must admit, tempers have flared and the scuffle has already begun. Then children need an opportunity to cool off before counseling begins. Some fight situations, but by no means all, need to be directed to the principal.

Disrespect to adults and defiance of authority are also areas which I feel it is necessary for the principal to handle. Children can be taught to respect authority. They will lead a much happier life by mastering this concept. The New Testament has a passage that instructs all of us in this area:

> Everyone must submit himself to the governing authorities, for there is no authority except that which God has established. The authorities that exist have been established by God. Consequently, he who rebels against the authority is rebelling against what God has instituted, and those who do so will bring judgment on themselves.
>
> *(Romans 13:1-2)*

Teachers need to be "the boss" in their classrooms. If they are allowed to send all of the behavior problems to the office, their authority is greatly undermined. I ask my new teachers what they think I can do when dealing with a behavior problem that they cannot do. Teachers are instructed to alert me when they become aware of students who are not conforming to the classroom behavior rules. Children should not be permitted to disrupt the class and distract the teacher from her primary purpose—teaching. When a student has worked through all of the steps (name on the board, check mark beside name—twice, etc.) in the classroom behavior plan, he rightly deserves a trip to the principal's office. His number is up! Generally, by this time the teacher will have contacted the parents and alerted me to the situation. Then, I am able to be the authority figure I need to be at my level.

There are myriads of types of behavior problems that have been referred to me, most of which could have been dealt with effectively right on the spot by the teacher or yard duty supervisor. These people do not want to take the time to talk to children. That is the main reason students are sent to the principal. Discipline is everyone's responsibility. I would like to give you an idea (and this is by no means an exhaustive list) of the types of behavior problems that have landed in my office. There is no rhyme or reason why the behaviors are listed in the order they occur.

Referrals from Classroom Teachers

Chewing gum
Pulling hair
Out of line
Talking
Slapping
Cutting hair
Wrestling
Not working
Arguing
Not minding
Hiding shoes
Leaning back in chair
Foot tapping
Name calling
Whistling
Doodling
Pencil fighting
Calling out dirty names
Not lining up

Entering room with muddy shoes
Copying from others
Jumping water puddles
Horsing around
Putting food coloring in mouth
Pulling chair out from under others
Taking other's things
Being out of assigned seat
Making weird noises
Killed a "pet" spider
Playing with toy
Placing "Kick Me" on others
Writing on the chalkboard
Reading rather than doing math
Throwing things

Referrals from Yard Duty Supervisors

Playing ball in restroom
Spitting
Skipping when told to walk
Bad language (or gestures)
Playing tag on the TOWER
Playing Tarzan on the
  TOWER
Throwing a ball up the slide
Listening to a Walkman Radio
Told joke to Yard duty & ran
Playing with water balloons
Doing cartwheels
Sitting on sink
Going "up" the slide
Being in the orchard
Splashing water on others

Writing on wall
Eating on the playground
Crowding in line
Wrestling
Kissing girls
Chasing girls
Using a water gun
Hiding things (hat, coat)
Buried hat in the sand
Playing tackle football
Standing on toilet
Popped a bag in cafeteria
Throwing "you name it"
Climbing over the fence
Stomping on a sand castle

Children quickly learn to play "hard ball" in dealing with adults. They exercise much more finesse than we give them credit for. I have listened to second grade children spin yarns so convincing the Tooth Fairy would believe them. Children have been caught "red handed" with multitudes of witnesses to proclaim their guilt and still maintained their innocence. Even their mothers believed them! Incidentally, mothers usually can tell when children are lying more quickly than anyone (at least from my experience). I guess I have heard about every reason, alibi, and excuse that was ever conceived. And kids have hundreds of them. Some of my favorite ones include:

- I don't know (or shrugging shoulders).
- He did it first.
- He told me to do it.

- My dad told me to fight . . . everytime.
- He wouldn't move.
- I accidentally kicked/hit him.
- I just tapped him lightly.
- We were just play fighting.
- She dared me to do it.
- He made me mad.
- After spitting on someone:
  "Something was caught in my throat."
- After biting someone:
  "We were playing "dogs and kitties."
- After cutting a boy's hair:
  "He dared me to do it."
- After climbing on sinks in restroom:
  "I was trying to see if the girls were peeking in at us."
- After kicking someone:
  "My foot just slipped."
- After stuffing a jacket in the toilet:
  "I thought it would flush down."
- After stealing lunches:
  "I was hungry."
  "Didn't you have breakfast?"
  "Yes, bacon and eggs, and toast and orange juice!"

The way you ask a question often determines the answer you get from a student. I'm sure they are not even aware of the word "semantics," but that doesn't hinder them from being an effective evader of the truth. Children try every kind of rationalization they can to keep from "owning up" to their responsibility in problem situations. Many times they mirror advice, comments, and/or information their parents have given them, which is fine as long as it doesn't conflict with rules at school and is sound advice. A few years ago, it seemed as if every student who came to my office told me his parents were going to have me fired, were going to sue me, or else I couldn't do anything to them because their parents had not signed the "permission to paddle" note (that was a good one). Parents really confuse their children when they advise them to fight whenever someone does something to them. It is difficult for a child to understand that he cannot fight at school when his parents are telling him to do so.

Most of the children who are sent to the office are reasonable. They have a good attitude and accept counseling. When you encounter a student who is argumentative, belligerent, or hostile, it is quite another matter. Even these students can be helped if they will listen. Much of it depends on their attitude. That's a tough one! I can't change attitudes. I can't make someone be responsible. But if a student is willing to listen, I can teach him some ways to problem solve that will work. The following plan (steps) works quite well with students who are willing to begin accepting some responsibility:

1. Ask the student to identify the problem. He needs to verbalize the reason he was sent to the office.
2. Ask him what he could have done differently in that particular situation.
3. Ask him what he is willing to try next time a similar situation occurs. You may need to give him some suggestions, but he must own them as his own.
4. Make a commitment to meet with him again shortly to check on his efforts. Several sessions will be necessary before these techniques become routine. Praise him even for small successes.

New teachers in particular need to develop a "bag of tricks" when dealing with children with problems. Some of the things I suggest to them (and they are certainly not original with me) include the following:

1. Set your standards the first day.

2. Discipline must be learned. Teach it.

3. Post your rules in the classroom.

4. Send a copy of your rules to parents (and discuss them at Back to School Night).

5. Personality, not knowledge, makes the difference in teaching.

6. When children misbehave:
   —Change their seat in the room.
   —Talk to the student outside the classroom door.
   —Isolate the offender.
   —Ignore minor infractions.
   —Be firm, fair, and friendly.
   —Call home!
   —Use a check system.
   —Be consistent.
   —Avoid threats.
   —Keep your sense of humor.

7. The more problems you learn to handle yourself, the more effective you will be. Constantly sending students to the office for discipline, erodes your authority.

I genuinely want to help children learn to problem solve—to think before they act! Along these lines, I have learned that little things make a big difference. When I'm on the playground, I try to take care of even the smallest complaint. You simply cannot let little things slide. If I don't do something, the problem generally comes back to me in the form of an argument, hitting, a fight, or what have you. Many times children just want you to listen. You don't have to do anything major to punish the offender. Most of the time I am able to use a little humor, the kids laugh, and go on about their job—playing. I teach children that it isn't being a "tattle-tale" to complain if someone does something to you that you don't like, or to tell on someone who is doing something wrong. To me, that is being a good citizen. Oh, sure, I realize there is a fine line here, and some children (especially first graders) get the idea that they need to tell you about every little thing. A little fine tuning works! It is also important to follow through. Children are surprised when I visit them outside their classroom door and request the note they were supposed to have parents sign.

The goal is to help children learn to take responsibility for their own behavior. Fortunately at my school, most children come from homes where parents have already provided a good foundation. Many of these children are more afraid of what their parents will do to them if they get in trouble than what the principal will do. Students in grades three and six were asked to write a composition titled "Reflections on a Visit to the Principal's Office." I would like to share some of their comments:

Third graders said:

- I would be scared because a math teacher might be in there.
- I would enjoy the visit and the pictures on the walls.
- I would say, "I think I am too young to die."
- I bet we would talk about the birds and the bees.
- If I had to visit the principal, I would have to think of an idea real fast.
- I would be a little suspicious.
- He would probably yell at me so loudly you could hear it all the way to Japan.
- I would be in big trouble with my mom and dad.
- The principal would tie me up, but I would get loose. He would lock me in the restroom, but I would crawl out the window.
- I would talk to the principal about school—how to raise money and how to improve the food in the cafeteria.

Sixth graders said:

- I think that principals should be "pals."
- I would be really embarrassed.
- What did I do to deserve it?
- I would be very proud of myself because I don't get into trouble.
- I would have a lot of butterflies in my stomach.
- I would be scared when the principal rolls his eyes.
- I wouldn't know what to expect. That's the hard part!
- Surely they got the wrong person!
- I would probably throw up all over the place.
- I would take my medicine.
- My skin would be crawling, and I would like to crawl too.
- The principal would chuckle and give me a reward.
- I would want to sink into the floor.
- I would feel like a protagonist in a horror show.

11

WHAT WORKS FOR ME

In an earlier chapter I wrote about the bees which pollinate the almond blossoms on the trees surrounding the school each spring. A "Bee Alert" is placed in the school newsletter, and children are cautioned to give the bees plenty of space. There are other kinds of "BE's" which I have found useful to be alert about also. These "Be Alert's," not necessarily presented in any certain order, guide me as I perform my duties as a principal.

BE YOURSELF

You are not going to fool anyone. The principal is vulnerable. He or she is exposed to the public constantly. Children are amazed when they see me in a supermarket or fast food place. I guess it is hard for them to believe that principals eat, buy groceries, and go to movies just like "real" people. I was so shy when I was growing up, I actually went out of my way (far, far out of my way!) to avoid people like teachers or principals or policemen. I don't know what I thought they were going to say or do to me.

When I became a principal (I'm talking about a REAL

principal, not a vice principal), I knew what kind of principal I did not want to be. I felt uncomfortable when someone called me "BOSS." I had no desire to be the boss. I wanted to be part of the TEAM. I wanted to work WITH the staff to deliver the best educational program possible to the children we served. I could not achieve this by being a pretender. I certainly did not want to intimidate people—not my staff, the parents, or the children. And, I did not want to be "the HEAVY." One of the things I have worked very hard to do is dispel the notion that the principal's office is a bad place to visit. Children come to my office to read to me, to receive awards, as members of committees to help solve problems, to share things, or just to visit.

BE POSITIVE

I learned some valuable lessons about being positive when I had the experience of working in a negative environment. When I was a vice principal, just about all I did all day long was deal with behavior problems. If I were not meeting with students in my office, I was handling their problems on the playground. I would become very depressed, and in those days, I did not look forward to school. Many of the children I dealt with had serious problems. They needed much more than I was able to give them. Sometimes I felt as if I was making good progress with some of the children. They seemed to be listening and responding to some of the problem-solving techniques I tried to share with them. Then there were mountains of problems with parents. I was the real "bad guy" who didn't like children (and especially their kid). And, I dealt with teachers who thought it was "cute" to joke with children, but "not cool" when the children tried to be funny with them. I'm talking about a kind of ridicule and sarcasm that would light your torch. How do you defend a teacher who tapes a child's mouth shut for talking too much?

It can't be done. I was embarrassed for the teacher. I could see so much wrong and so little right at the school, but I was virtually powerless to change it.

The leader makes all the difference in the world. During my elementary and junior high years there were winning football teams at the high school. The coach was an outstanding leader. He knew how to motivate and inspire his players. The first year I went out for varsity football, there was a new coach. He smoked the biggest cigars I've ever seen, every other word out of his mouth was profanity, and he humiliated me. I quit, for a number of reasons, the main one being that I just wasn't good enough. The team only won one game that year after having gone to the state championship the year before. I think the coach might have humiliated some of his good players too.

I attend a very active, growing church. The pastor is recognized across the state and nation as a great leader. I believe the greatness of his administrative talent lies in his ability to share himself. He started an intern program to train young men for ministry. Many who were trained under his leading now serve as pastors and missionaries throughout the world. He leads by example.

A former principal of the district junior high school was my supervisor for a number of years before he became the superintendent. He taught me more than any man I have ever known. He had a positive attitude and successfully led the district during a time when enrollment doubled. He was widely recognized in the community and in the state for his leadership abilities. He would say, "Always do what's best for kids." Or, "We're here to help people (teachers, staff) improve, not to get rid of them." He took a personal interest in his employees' welfare.

People like my pastor and superintendent have a positive outlook on life. Being successful whether it be as a coach, pastor, educator, or what-have-you is not easy. Each profession can be stressful. But the leader makes the difference. If you look for trouble, sure enough, it will find you. On the other hand, if you maintain a positive attitude, you will put your enemies at ease. A verse in the Bible (Proverbs 3: 6) helps me to focus on being positive:

> "Trust in the Lord with all your heart, and lean not to your own understanding. In all your ways acknowledge Him, and He will make your paths straight."

Years ago I would answer the telephone knowing it was a hostile parent, and be on the defense from the very beginning of the conversation. An irate parent would come to see me, and I would immediately tighten up and be ready for a fight (verbal fight, that is). My mouth would become dry, my hands would shake, I would bite my nails, and I sat with my knees close together so they wouldn't knock. Then I figured out that it wasn't my problem. I wasn't the one who had been sent to the office for fighting. I didn't tear the kid's jacket, I didn't spit out the bus window and get a bus citation, and I certainly hadn't pulled the kindergarten girl's pants down. So, why was I so defensive? The person who coined the expression, "Have a nice day," must have been a positive person. It is not easy to carry all of the burdens of administration around and be a nice guy all the time, but with practice and a little experience it can be done.

BE PREPARED

I have to write things down. If I am talking to two students who were sent to the office for fighting, I take notes on what they tell me. When I talk to a parent who is upset with a teacher or with the way her child was treated, I take notes. At the Superintendent's Council meetings, I write notes on the agenda. I try to maintain a journal of major events (an upset parent is an example of a major event.) that happened during the day so that I can recall the information if needed.

Sometimes it is wise to "buy time" so that you can prepare. The secretary pulls a child's cumulative record for me when a parent has scheduled a conference with me. I go over report card grades, test scores, health information, and talk to the teacher before the conference. When I have been away from school all afternoon at a meeting and return to my office, many times there are telephone messages for me to return. Unless there are urgent calls to make, I sometimes wait until the following day to return the calls. This practice allows parents who were very angry to "cool down." Many parents have admitted that they were very angry when they called, but had time to think about the situation and realized there must be another side to the story. They are then willing to hear the other side, and in the meantime, I have had an opportunity to find out what the other side of the story was.

The way you say things makes a big difference. It helps to rehearse what you are going to say. Sounds funny, but it's true. If you fail to prepare what you will say, it will come out wrong. Principals are misquoted often enough without our making the situation worse. When a parent calls the superintendent to complain about a decision I have made, he reads from "his notes" what the parent has said. More often then not, the parent has either misquoted me or has made assumptions that were not true. For example, a parent called the superintendent complaining that I would not move her child to another teacher's classroom at the school because the other classes were full. She was upset because I told her that her child might need to be transferred to another school in the district. Only the superintendent can do that.

When the superintendent called me, I explained that the parent had come to see me because she wanted her child moved immediately. I went through many reasons why I did not feel it would be wise to move the girl to another teacher's classroom at the same school. I asked her to consider letting me talk with the teacher to get her perspective. I also wanted to meet with the girl. I requested that we wait two weeks before doing anything. If things were not better in two weeks, I told the mother, I would like to meet with her again to decide what would be the best course of action to take for her daughter. She had called the superintendent one week after meeting with me. She told him that she thought I was brushing her off (I spent almost an hour with her), and she felt that I would not call her back. The superintendent asked me to call her, and I did. She graciously allowed me to "re-explain" my position and agreed to wait until the end of the week before making a decision.

During the following weeks, I met three times with her daughter and twice with the teacher. The girl admitted, even after the first week, that she had been unhappy because she was several weeks behind in her work and the teacher was putting pressure on her to get it caught up. Her father had conferenced with the teacher just prior to the winter break, found out she was far behind in her work, and was not too happy with her. She did catch up during the two weeks and agreed that things were much better.

When I called the mother that final time, she admitted that her daughter seemed to be much happier in class, had caught up on all the work, but she would still prefer that her daughter be moved. I don't think it would have mattered if I had waited two days, two weeks, or two months in this case. She definitely was not going to accept any other decision. She wanted her daughter moved.

The previous year a parent made a similar request which I also denied. The parent went to the president of the school board demanding that the child be moved. The superintendent called me with a direct order to move the child. Not necessary to explain—just move the boy. He did come to school and meet with the teacher to explain that "the move" was not to be construed as a reflection of her teaching ability.

I was not about to go through that experience again—not for the teacher, and not for me. I talked with the girl's teacher and explained the situation. I also talked to the teacher who would be receiving the child the next week. And so, the girl was moved. It was not a pleasant experience. In my opinion, the girl came out the loser. She will meet another teacher somewhere in her school experience who will require her to mature and accept responsibility. Since she chose to "run from the problem" this time, she will probably do it again. She had an excellent teacher who was providing her with the structure she needed to grow and mature.

BE ORGANIZED

Organization is important! You can save yourself many headaches by being organized. My secretary makes fun of me because I'm so organized. Rarely is there a stack of papers on my desk—unless she arranges the mail in neat piles all around my desk as a joke. She loves to do that at the end of the day or when I'm gone to a meeting. I have a pleasant surprise when I come to work the next day. Other administrators accuse me of hiding everything in the drawers. Not so. Everyone has his own style. I simply find it difficult to function when my desk is cluttered. I'm always impressed when I visit a principal whose desk is cluttered, and he or she can go through all of that "stuff" and immediately find a memo or report. Bravo! But not for me. The old adage that you should never handle a piece of paper twice is not bad advice.

How do people learn to be organized? Is one born with that talent? Who knows! Organization has always been a strong point with me. When I was in my preteen years, we had a walk-in pantry. My parents would buy tons of canned goods (on sale of course), and I loved to organize the cans on the tall shelves. Every can had to be right side up, labels facing front, with all the different types of cans clustered together, and WOE to the one who messed them up. Even today everything in my room has a place, and everything is in its place. Opposites attract, so luckily the whole house doesn't have "my personality".

This age of technology has improved my ability to organize and saves a great deal of time. I have always enjoyed typing and with the advent of word processing on a computer, I like it even more. When I first became an administrator, the superintendent did not want his principals using typewriters. This was before computers were so abundant. He preferred that we use a hand-held tape recorder and let the secretary do the typing from a recorder. The theory was that this practice would save us time. We could use the tape recorder in our office to note discipline cases immediately, in the car while traveling to a meeting, and even carry a mini-recorder in our pocket and record things at home. I found it interesting that this whole philosophy changed when computers came along. The superintendent not only had a computer in his office, but he requested that the governing board purchase a matching one for his home so that he could work on reports there too. My computer (I have one at home, too) and I are very good friends.

When I go into a teacher's classroom to do an observation, I take nothing on which to write. Depending on the situation, I spend from thirty minutes to an hour in a classroom. I return to my office and write up the evaluation using my computer word processor. The format is usually the same, and I can complete the two-page evaluation in about thirty minutes. Copies are run off on the photocopy machine and placed in the teacher's mailbox within the hour. If I had to rely on taking notes, coming back to my office to tape record the observation, give the recorded report to the secretary, and wait until she could find time (I don't know about your secretary, but mine is too busy already!) to type it, the teacher might not know what I said for days. It is important to me that the teachers receive feedback quickly. When I was an English teacher, I always made it a practice to return work students turned in just as quickly as possible—usually the next day, and that's hard on English teachers.

BE A PROBLEM PREVENTER

Many of us wait for problems to occur and then work frantically to find ways to solve them. It makes more sense to work from the other side—to think things through so that problems do not develop. This concept is certainly not new, and it did not originate with me. Of course, many problems simply cannot be prevented despite all of our best efforts.

If the principal was away at a meeting when I served as a vice principal, I had the absolute authority to "declare a rainy day." Such power! Around mid-morning one day I announced that it was a "Rainy Day" which meant that teachers must remain in their classrooms with students. Students are sent in "waves" to the restrooms. Teachers, if they are lucky, are "spelled" by anyone available from vice principal to librarian. Well, a few minutes after I had declared the rainy day, you guessed it, the rain stopped. Teachers began calling to request permission to let their children go to recess. Of course, I verified that it was indeed not raining any more (After all I do have a master's degree so I can make those kinds of decisions.), so I agreed that the students should take their recess break. As soon as they disgorged from the classrooms, a HEAVY downpour occurred. You know who received credit for that decision! I decided if I lived long enough to become a principal, I would never declare rainy days. This is a no-win type of situation. At my school now I have given up that wonderful power. Teachers look out the window to see if it is raining, and then they know what to do. Well, it works most of the time. Once in awhile I still hear the secretary respond to a question when a teacher calls on a rainy day with, "If it's raining, it's a rainy day".

Train your staff. When new teachers are assigned to schools in my district, they receive a full day of in-service orientation at the district level. Then I usually spend two or three lengthy sessions with the new teachers and assign them a "buddy" at their grade level to help them with routines and procedures. Each teacher is given a *NEW TEACHER HANDBOOK* (I wrote it the first year I was at Stanislaus.) which we go through carefully. This procedure prevents lots of problems. When I began my teaching career, no one pointed out where the restrooms were located—much less the ditto machine, where to go for supplies, or which forms were appropriate to use.

Follow through quickly. I have mentioned before that it is important for teachers to have the materials they need to do their job. Part of my job is seeing to it that they have these materials. When I was a vice principal, this was a major part of my job, and having just come from the classroom, I knew how important it was to have materials available for teachers. Fortunately, I have an administrative aide who has taken over this responsibility. She does an excellent job in this area because she knows that it is a high priority with me. It is a frustrating experience for teachers when there are not enough supplies or textbooks for their students. You really have problems then!

Keep your word. Don't make promises you can't keep. A new teacher I hired a few years ago came to me several times during the first two weeks of school requesting things for her room (supplies, repairs, books). This was before I had an administrative aide, so I filled the requests as quickly as I could. I became "somewhat" frustrated when I heard her ask (I have big ears) the secretary when the principal was going to do such and such. The fault was mostly mine. She had worked for principals who "took forever" to take care of a request, forgot it completely, or needed constant reminders. If I had covered my own philosophy about the importance of getting things done quickly for teachers during the training session, I would have alleviated her concern. She has learned that her requests will be taken care of quickly if it is at all within my power to do so.

I would like to make just one more point under the heading of "being a problem preventer." Administrators, just like parents, must clearly define the limits. If you do not set limits, you get what you deserve. When we as a staff have a problem or issue to work on, I need to set the perimeters before they begin discussing solutions or plans. There are usually some constraints or boundaries they need to know. Knowing the limits does not need to stifle creativity, and it certainly keeps the district office away.

They do not all turn out nicely. I remember one father who literally came storming past the secretary into my office with his wife and son close behind. The black man was at least six foot, five inches tall and weighed around 230 pounds. He towered over the desk in my direction with his hands wide apart. I could tell he wanted my attention! I asked him to be seated so that we could discuss the problem. He let me know that he would rather remain standing—which he did for the next hour or so.

His son had received his third bus citation which meant that he would not be permitted to ride the school bus for ten school days. He had received this particular citation for spitting on others. Parents always want to know what happened to "the other guy." If their child is punished, the other guy had better get the same treatment. Sounds fair! However, in this case, son said he did not spit. The "white" bus driver and the "white" kids on the bus just didn't like him, and wanted him to get into trouble.

The situation calmed down considerably, and I felt that they left in good spirits and with a lot better attitude. I had agreed to set up a meeting with the bus driver who wrote the citation, her supervisor, and myself for the next morning. The family left my office and went straight to the district office to see the superintendent. They entered his office the same way they had entered mine. He wasn't too impressed. But now, in addition to being upset with the bus driver, the teachers, and the students at school, the man was also most upset with that "white" honky principal who "claimed he was God almighty" (their words). I tried to remember how they could have come away with a direct quotation like that. The closest thing I could remember saying was that the principal had to be in control of his school—even what happens on the bus. Later, this family returned for the meeting I had scheduled with the bus driver and her boss. The driver related that the boy had spit, not once but many times. Other students who were sitting nearby were called into the office and verified her story in the family's presence. My investigation revealed that this family had left a trail of similar-type actions in several school districts in the state. The bus citation stuck, and he did not ride the bus for ten days.

This was not the end of the story, however. Toward the end of that school year (I'm talking about months later), the superintendent received a long document from the step-mother of this boy. The letter stated that black families were not treated with respect in this school district and at my school in particular. She had hired a lawyer to help her in this case of outright racial prejudice. Copies of the letter had been sent to thirty different individuals and organizations. Such people as Jesse Jackson and Monroe Taylor received copies along with "Sixty Minutes" and "20-20." I waited anxiously for a call from "Sixty Minutes." I figured they would want to interview this rogue principal. The call never came.

BE HONEST

Honesty is the best policy for sure. Encouraging children to tell the truth when they have already developed a habit of lying is very difficult. I let children know that I will respect them and believe that they are telling me the truth until I find out otherwise. Many children "box" themselves into a corner and cannot work their way out. They tell one lie to cover up for another one, and soon there is no wriggle room left.

When dealing with parents and staff, it is important to share information—to have no "hidden agendas." Many problems may be prevented by simply being honest with people. My school is old. The first wing was built in 1956. For several years we have been in line for remodeling. A school bond was passed to help achieve that goal. The remodeling has been delayed for many reasons. Parents who assisted in the passage of the bond who have children at the school do not understand the delay. Teachers have been working under extremely poor conditions for years and do not understand why no progress has been made several years after the bond passed. This is a very sensitive issue right now. The state highway which runs in front of the school is scheduled to become a major, six-lane freeway which will skirt the city of Modesto within five years. The first projections indicated this freeway expansion was at least twenty years in the future. Remodeling the existing buildings knowing that the highway work may be done in five years totally changes the picture. Keeping the school community informed on issues such as this is crucial. In this situation the principal is "caught in the middle." The task of "keeping everyone happy" falls on him, and he may not have all the facts or the latest information. Parents may deduce that there is more going on than meets the eye.

BE HUMOROUS

One of the greatest assets a teacher or administrator can have going for him is a good sense of humor. Recognizing the humor in situations and using it effectively to your advantage has the potential to diffuse many problems.

Several years ago the parent of a first grade youngster complained that the perfume worn by her child's teacher caused the child to have breathing problems. She discussed the situation with the teacher but did not feel that the teacher was sympathetic to her child's problem. The parent met with me to lodge her complaint about the perfume. She objected on grounds that the perfume was too strong. Evidently she did not object to the brand of perfume worn by the teacher. I told her I would conduct a "sniff" test to determine whether the perfume was offensive. For the next few days when I visited this teacher's room, I made it a point to sniff vigorously; however, I could not conclusively say that I even smelled perfume. I know that the teacher was not purposely doing anything differently. She assured me that she was still wearing the same perfume, and she didn't intend to switch. I didn't see any reason for her to change perfumes.

A kindergarten teacher came to school just before Christmas vacation wearing a string of colored Christmas tree lights around her neck which blinked on and off. She loaned them to me, and I entertained children all morning with humorous comments about the lights and gave them crazy reasons for why I was all lit up.

At Halloween (not my favorite) I dress up in a costume and lead the parade. The children really enjoy seeing their principal dressed like General Patton (my favorite one), Big Bird, a gorilla, Spiderman, a monk, and this year—a dog. I always make sure the secretary takes a picture of me at the desk answering the telephone or looking very busy. After the parade, I quickly change into my regular clothes and go back to visit the classrooms. Children ask me if I was the . . . I tell them I could not have been the one. I was in my office working!

BE CONSISTENT

Little things make a big difference. If I tell a student he will serve a one-hour, in-school suspension, I make sure he spends that much time and not any more than that. If the faculty meeting is scheduled to begin at 2:30, we begin at 2:30—whether everyone is there or not. When teachers request textbooks or other materials, I make every effort to see that the things they requested are delivered quickly. At the site level it is not possible to control payment of bills ordered on school purchase orders; however, I always make sure that the purchase orders are sent from my office to the business office for payment as quickly as possible.

In counseling with children, so many of them tell me that adults they have met don't seem to care. The adults don't listen, and they fail many times to follow through. Students are surprised when I call them back into the office or visit them outside their classroom door to see if they have returned a form letter I gave them the day before for a parent signature. They are supposed to return the letter to the office, but many forget—like they forget to do homework, feed the dog, take out the trash, or clean their room. If the letter is not returned, I end up calling parents, but I would rather the child take the responsibility to go home and share the problem with his parents.

If you tell someone you are going to do something, make every effort to keep your word. I have found that if I treat people with respect, they will respect me.

BE A GOOD LISTENER

As an elementary teacher I very seldom had conferences with the principal, but at the junior high level once in awhile I needed to talk to someone. I remember going to the principal on several occasions. However, when I saw the pattern developing, I stopped going and worked the problems out the very best I could. When I would go to this principal for help, I would briefly share the problem with him. That's about the last opportunity I had to speak. He would always relate experiences he had, and they would usually be far worse than I was sharing, or else I failed to see the relevance of what he was relating at all. I usually left with no solution and more frustrated than before I went to see him.

One morning around 7:30 the kindergarten teachers came to see me. I can always tell when these ladies are coming to share a problem. They sat down and began relating their "concerns." I listened, and listened, and listened! Oh, once in awhile I would interject a word of wisdom, but mostly I just listened to them. When all the issues had been presented, they thanked me and got up to leave. I asked them why they were thanking me. I certainly hadn't done anything! They just needed to talk and, more importantly, they needed someone to listen and understand.

Talking on the telephone to a parent who is upset is one of the most difficult things to do. I would much rather be face to face with the person. I have to restrain myself to keep from "jumping in" to the conversation too soon when someone is talking to me on the phone. A little patience goes a long way in these cases. I think this situation is similar to the one teachers face when they have been teaching for many years and sometimes try to take short cuts, leave out steps, or forget that the learning is new for this group. The concepts must be presented slowly and sequentially until students understand. It is better to let the person completely tell his story before responding with your own information or opinions.

BE GONE

Spend time away from your work doing things you enjoy. When you are away from work, be really gone! Easy to say, hard to do! Many weekends I work at school on Saturday and

Sunday. On week days I arrive at work an hour before teachers have to report. There are many night meetings. When summer vacation finally arrives, it takes me a couple of weeks just to unwind and leave school behind.

I attend one or two major conferences each year. This time away from school helps me to do a better job when I return. I enjoy jogging, and have even taken up long distance running. When I jog at the junior college track, I use the time to problem solve, pray, and think. It is excellent therapy. I don't have the greatest voice, but I enjoy singing in the choir at my church. We have rehearsals once a week and sing in two worship services on Sunday morning. The choir also produces musicals which require long rehearsals. I enjoy participating in them. When I really want to forget everything, I go to a movie. And, the most fun of all to me is reading. I enjoy reading historical fiction. Sometimes I have two or three books going at a time.

Retirement will sneak up on us before we know it, so we must not put off developing other interests besides our work at school. We all have to develop our own talents and know ourselves well enough so that we pursue hobbies that will fulfill us. It is difficult to find time to develop these interests when we are so busy with school, but it is important to make time. One principal I know studies the stock market and invests his money. He also does well with real estate ventures. I do not want to retire and become so bored that I need to take a job washing cars, pumping gas, or working in a convenience store to keep me occupied. Hopefully some of my interests will carry over into retirement. When I'm gone, I want to be really gone.

12

IT'S REALLY THE PRINCIPLE!

If you are considering becoming a superintendent or have ambitions toward a career in the district office, you might want to skip this chapter. I do not consider myself a rebel or a person who "makes waves," but there are times when I feel that it is important to take a stand. It's the principle of the thing! Some of the situations I describe will seem petty perhaps, but they were issues about which I felt I must take a stand.

When you are a new employee just beginning the job, you would like for things to go well. And it would be nice if the boss liked you. Well, I was a new junior high school English teacher with the first month of teaching under my belt and a pay check in sight . . . or, so I thought. In my mailbox at school one afternoon I had a note from the superintendent stating that I would not receive my pay check because I had not completed my tuberculosis test (TB test). I was in shock. I had a family to feed. I had visions of my children starving. I could just see my three little children in rags and my wife going around barefoot (or did she do that anyway?). The landlord would probably throw my pregnant wife, my children, the dog, and me out on the street for nonpayment of the rent. I worried and fussed about it all evening. Then I made a decision.

I typed out a long position paper which I presented to the superintendent the next day. It wasn't that easy; I was scared to death. In the paper I stated that I felt it was important for the district to inform new employees that they would not be paid if a TB clearance were not on file. Further, a condition such as this should be written on the employee's contract specifying the date the TB clearance must be submitted and that there would be no warrant until it was received in the office. Districts need to provide new employees with proper orientation. No training sessions at all were provided by the district at that time. The letter I submitted was, in fact, my resignation. Later I learned that there were several other employees in the district who had also received notices that they would not be paid due to the lack of a TB test. To make a long story short, all of us received our pay checks. Each year following that incident there was a notation on all employees' contracts letting them know about this rather minor little condition of employment. The district also began an extensive orientation program for new teachers. On the other hand, if the superintendent had not been a reasonable man and really concerned about his employees, he would have accepted my resignation with no regrets.

I was on the Board of Deacons at my church many years ago. My area of responsibility was missions. The church had just gone through a rough time. A dynamic new pastor took the lead, and it wasn't long before the church began to grow. The deacons held regular monthly meetings which were conducted like those of a large corporation. In many churches it is almost a routine, cut and dried, doesn't-even-have-to-be-discussed matter to reduce giving to mission projects if funds are in short supply. A certain amount of money had been budgeted for missions, but it appeared that the board was going to reduce that amount significantly. In my most emotional manner, I let it be known that the missions budget should not be cut. I made quite a scene, I'm afraid. The pastor took me aside later and thanked me for saying what I felt. He said he knew I was working hard and that missions were important to me. And, he hoped the other board members would learn a lesson from the zeal I displayed. God surely didn't need my help, but it was the principle of the thing! Giving to missions has never been slighted by my church.

I had all kinds of moonlighting jobs when I first started teaching, but my first love was teaching. I took on the other jobs in order to survive—you know, eat, buy clothes, pay rent. The evolution to year round schools came about too late for me! I also taught summer school. One year I was teaching math to primary students. I say primary students because ages of the children ranged from six to nine. Some would be entering first grade in the fall while the older children would be in grade four. The task was to keep everyone busy at their identified instructional level. I think that was the year I began losing my hair? There was one little guy in the class who just would not behave. I had tried many tactics from my "bag of tricks" but nothing worked. One day I had the boy stand outside the classroom in front of the window where I could keep an eye on him. The principal walked by, saw the boy standing there, and marched him back into the room. Without saying a word to me or the boy, she turned and left the room. I was fairly furious! She had made it clear that students were not to be sent to the office (she was too busy for that.), and yet my use of this "time out" was not acceptable either. Well, the next time Jack misbehaved he was right back outside the door. If the principal had certain expectations about how to discipline children (i.e., doesn't want them standing outside), she needed to clearly convey her expectations to the teachers. She certainly made no points with me by undermining my authority. The principal must provide support and training for staff on an ongoing basis. From that experience I learned that a principal is first and foremost a teacher. I always spend time with new teachers and student teachers who are working at my school by providing instruction regarding good discipline techniques, among other things.

During the 1960's America was going through a period of permissiveness unsurpassed by any society in the world at the time. The schools in America didn't escape either. This was the time when "new" math was introduced, and students were "free to be" whatever. We had just moved into a new building which had very few internal walls. The entire middle section was open. In three sections of this area English teachers were on display. In the other corner the Spanish teacher did her thing—verbally for the most part. It was exciting! Students would wave at their friends in the adjacent area, notes were passed via paper airplanes, and teachers did a lot of shouting (to be heard). There were other classes like math and science going on around the perimeter.

This was the time to experiment. The situation certainly couldn't be any worse. Many schools in the country were having tremendous success with paraprofessionals at that time. It was decided at the governing board level that the math and English departments would conduct a "pilot" paraprofessional program for one year. I was the head of the English Department. I selected and hired three paraprofessionals to work with me. These were young ladies who had either just completed college or at least had some college background. One actually had a teaching credential but did not want the responsibility of a full time job. These paraprofessionals were each assigned groups of children. I designed the curriculum, made presentations to large groups (three classes meeting together), evaluated the paraprofessionals and the students, met with parents, handled discipline problems, and generally served as director of the whole operation.

I was also working on my master's degree at the time. In one of the education classes we were assigned a paper to write. I chose to write about the paraprofessional program. In the paper I discussed the history of the paraprofessional program, the positive and negative aspects I had observed, how students reacted to it, and some of the problems I had personally encountered with the program at my school. The following story generated lots of laughs in the Education Department at the college.

I considered myself a fairly conservative-type individual. I believed in baseball, Ford, and apple pie. I also thought it was a good idea for young ladies to wear bras. But, this was the sixties! Many, many women chose to be liberated at that time. Had I told the young women I hired that part of their job description included wearing a bra? Wasn't I the person who came so unglued when my boss didn't properly inform me of expected standards? What gave me the idea that I could demand that girls wear bras? Besides, I didn't want to be the one to tell them. So, I went to my principal with the problem. When he finished laughing, we discussed possible strategies to deal with the "bra-less" paraprofessional teachers. There were many young ladies looking up (and too many young men looking down) to these teachers. Many of the students were upset when their models decided to quit rather than wear a bra. Well, it really was the principle of the thing!

There are times when it would be better for a person to change jobs or professions rather than remain in an occupation or work place and not be able to be the person he needs to be. I know a teacher who was absolutely unwilling to change or adapt when strict regulations about religion were imposed by the state and federal governments as the result of court decisions. This teacher played the guitar and led the class in singing religious songs. Hymns and other camp-type music were played on the record player. Kindergarten children said "grace" before having their morning snack. Despite verbal and written warnings, this teacher chose to continue with these practices. Of course, the administration would not stand for this behavior. Pressure was brought to bear, and the person is no longer a teacher.

When is it important to take a stand? At what point do you decide that the job you are doing with children is more important than the "display" of religious activities or openly sharing your testimony while on the job? Is it a "cop out" when one does not share his testimony during working hours and try to be effective by the example set and the life lived in the presence of children each day? These are serious questions for persons with strong religious convictions. However, the Bible teaches that we are to respect those in authority over us. God has placed the principal in charge of the school just as He has positioned the superintendent at the district office and assigned each teacher to a class. He has also allowed the court decisions that separate church and state. Therefore, if I want to teach or be an administrator in a public school, I must abide by the rules and regulations that exist. I know many fine Christian teachers in the public schools who radiate their faith by the very life they live. They do make a difference in children's lives.

Then there are times when you can't win for losing. One time at the Superintendent's Council, which is attended by all of the principals in the district, we were discussing new attendance procedures. Attendance accounting had recently been programmed for the district computer. Each of the sites had a computer terminal which mainframed to the district office. Secretaries were provided with training sessions so that they could learn this new system. The business manager asked us to talk with our secretaries and share our concerns with him regarding this new system. My secretary was totally frustrated with this highly complex operation. Following my discussion with her, I drafted a report to the business manager outlining her concerns. The business manager paid me a visit shortly after receiving my report. He was upset because I was not being "part of the team." I was bucking the system and making his job harder. The report was critical, but it was an honest appraisal of the problems and concerns my secretary had expressed to me. I erred in not understanding how things really were. What the district office wanted to know was that things were working fine! I can do that—to a point.

This last summer water tests of the deep well at Stanislaus School revealed that the water quality was poor—almost to the critical level (a reading below 2.5 is considered unsafe). The school is outside the city limits so there is no sewer system or water supply other than that provided by wells. The school is surrounded by farms, and the farmers have been using pesticides on their fields for years. These contaminants have seeped deeper and deeper into the soil, finally reaching the water table. The tests of our well were in the "safe" zone, but just barely. The business manager and superintendent called me to the district office to explain the situation. I was directed to "keep this quiet." They told me that only two people in the district knew of this problem besides myself, and they didn't want it to go any further. I didn't sleep well that night. This conversation occurred a few days before school opened. How could I remain silent? If there were even the slightest hint that the drinking water was unsafe, I could not in good conscience remain silent. The superintendent visited my school the next day. Even though he tried to assure me that the water was safe to drink, I was not convinced, and I voiced my concerns. I felt that the public, the parents of children at the school, should know about the problems with the well. There was no disagreement between the superintendent and me at this point. We talked about the possibility of bringing in bottled water, but he stated that it was not necessary at the time. Later that year bottled water was used until the filtration system was working.

It wasn't long after that meeting that an article appeared in the local newspaper. The superintendent had arranged a meeting with a representative from the newspaper, a county health inspector, the personnel director, and the business manager to discuss the situation and arrange to print an article in the newspaper to assure the public that the water was safe and that the district was taking the initiative to solve the problem before it became critical. An excellent, well-written article appeared in the newspaper the next day. The article used the analogy of a postage stamp to a football field in comparing the amount of water one must drink to become ill. The well water would be tested each month to determine if corrective action needed to be taken. No one in the area was able to locate a filtering system large enough to handle the volume of a commercial-type water system of this size. So far the water remains safe to drink, and the district is investigating ways to solve the problem by filtering, digging a new well, or making the existing well deeper. I was greatly relieved, and my confidence restored in district officials, when they decided to share this information with the public. God placed my bosses over me, and I have a responsibility to support their decisions and to work with them.

Principals who have an active parent organization are fortunate indeed. I have such a group! The parent organization at Stanislaus School is not affiliated with the national Parent Teacher Association (PTA). We are an independent group known as the Parents' Club. The principal of the school always serves as the "Adviser" to this group which meets monthly. We stopped participating in such fund-raising activities as carnivals and spaghetti feeds many years ago. Now we have one major fund raiser each year—the annual jogathon. Some years, one hundred percent of the students have participated. The jogathon nets over $12,000 in a good year. There have been some good years!

In many schools it is difficult to find parents interested enough to fill the offices, serve as room mothers, publish a monthly newsletter, and chair the various committees. This is certainly not the case at Stanislaus School. Meetings are generally well attended. Parents are interested in what is happening at their school. Proceeds from our jogathon are used to benefit all of the children at school. Many mothers have served as the president of the Parents' Club since I have been principal, and each of them has been keenly interested in making Stanislaus School the best school possible. Meetings are conducted in a highly professional manner. Most presidents serve a one-year term of office; however, there have been a few who served two-year terms. The membership changes each year as children graduate and move on to the junior high, new parents move to our area, or parents with new kindergarten children begin school.

A few times we have had some surprises at our meetings. I do not feel that an open parent club meeting is the place to discuss problems a parent may be having with a teacher. Nor is this meeting a place to air personal gripes. That kind of business needs to be discussed with the principal in private. When a parent new to the school begins talking about a teacher (and it has happened), I direct them to make an appointment to see me privately about their concerns. It usually works out very well. The good reputation of teachers can be destroyed quickly by rumors or false information too freely shared.

In all the years I have worked with parents' groups there has just been one major disagreement between us. When I first became principal, I started a "Student of the Month" program. So, what's new, you say? We all do that! Teachers chose two students each month to be their students of the month. I took pictures of each child (pictures are done by our school photographer now), which the secretary mounts on a seasonal background and displays on a large bulletin board in the hallway. At our monthly awards assembly each student of the month is called up front to receive a certificate. Names are published in the monthly parent newsletter, and all of the children who have received this honor throughout the year are treated to a gigantic picnic at one of the local parks at the end of the school year. Separate trips are planned for primary and intermediate children.

Sounds great, so where is the disagreement? It seems that many parents felt that if all of the children in the school couldn't be selected to be a student of the month, the program should be dropped. They felt that it was unfair and unnecessarily hurtful to the ones who were not selected. I maintained that any student who met the criteria established by teachers (with input from the parent organization) would be selected as a student of the month. Teachers are not limited to the selection of only two children per month. Some children do not meet the qualifications to be a student of the month. A student must be responsible, dependable, friendly, a good worker, and have a positive attitude to qualify. These qualities are not "watered down" or taken lightly by teachers. There are months when a teacher may not choose anyone to be a student of the month. Toward the end of the school year a teacher may select four students for a particular month. This is the way real life is. There are other awards for children who are not selected to be a student of the month, such as "Most Improved Student," which is also a monthly award that a student may earn for either academics or behavior. And, hopefully, a student may improve enough to be selected by his teacher as a student of the month.

One year parents voted not to support the Student of the Month program. They discussed the program after I had left the meeting. They felt that it discriminated against children who could never be selected. Perhaps they were right, but I could not see that stopping a successful program which involved over three hundred students was the answer either. Children always looked forward to the hot dogs, ice cream, and other goodies the parents provided for our picnics. When their support was withdrawn, I funded the event with student body candy sale money. The Student of the Month program is strongly supported by teachers, it wasn't a parent club activity *per se,* and I feel that it is one of the most rewarding things we do.

There are other times when a principal must stand by his convictions. Many parents want to choose their child's teacher each year. If you are just beginning in administration, beware of this one. Certainly there are times when the parent may enlighten the principal about medical history, sensitivity, need for a father figure, or other information he may use to make a good decision about placement. The principal needs to be sensitive to parents in this area and will probably make better decisions if he listens carefully. Some principals may make it a practice to allow parents to choose their child's teachers. Many times the reason given by parents for wanting to select the teacher has more to do with who the other children are in the teacher's class. Parents and children see the computer printout posted on the windows in front of the school a few weeks before school opens, and when the child's friends are not in his group, the child convinces the parent that a move is absolutely essential in order for him to receive a good education. Moving a child so that friends can be together is not a good reason to give the principal to move a child.

Once the school year is under way, there will always be a few parents who would like to move their child to another teacher. It's funny how this usually occurs near report card time, either when progress reports are sent home or when the report card is actually given to parents. Suddenly there is a huge personality clash between the child and the teacher. The child usually reports to his parents that the teacher is "picking on him," doesn't like him, or will not explain any of the work when he doesn't understand how to do it. I wonder if the parents aren't ever just a little bit curious when they consider all of the missing assignments. Until recently, I have never moved a child from one teacher to another at my school, and then it was not my decision. I think this is a bad practice. It is devastating to the teacher whose self confidence is shattered to pieces. This practice also opens "Pandora's box" as other children get the idea that all they have to do is complain to their parents about a teacher, and the principal will have to move them. Sometimes moving a child from a teacher's room is a good idea, but the transfer needs to be to another school in the district.

The longer you are an administrator, the more "war stories" you will have to share. If you are wise, you will learn from your experiences. Did you ever wonder why the principalship is considered a "middle management" position? A principal needs to be a good juggler. Many times you will be caught in the middle between district office personnel and teachers, teachers and parents, teachers and students, and sometimes even students and their parents. Your future as an administrator may very well depend on your ability to balance all of these acts.

I picked up a catchy little phrase somewhere which makes sense. It goes like this: "If you think straight, you will act right." As difficult as the job has become (and it is becoming increasingly more so), there are many rewards. A principal must definitely be a strong, self-assured individual who is willing to stand up for his principles.

13

TEACHERS MAKE THE DIFFERENCE

School is a complex operation. It isn't exactly like when we were children playing school with one person being the teacher (holding a switch to paddle us with, no doubt) and the rest of us sitting on the grass under a shade tree listening dutifully to her talking. That's what teachers do, right? No, wrong! Not the teachers I work with anyway. Neither is school like it was one hundred years ago with the little red school house where teachers were responsible for reading, 'riting, and 'rithmetic. It isn't even like it was when I began my teaching career twenty-seven years ago with little preparation. School officials in Texas were desperate for teachers. I believe they would have hired any "warm body" who walked in the door.

Everyone who works at school is important—from the bus drivers who transport the children to the custodian who secures the buildings the last thing every evening. The task of educating the children would be impossible without each one doing his job. We are all part of the team. But, teachers make the biggest difference regarding the education a child receives.

We have all read or seen lists of rules that pertained to

teaching or teachers many years ago. Reading these rules today provides us with a good laugh. These rules of long ago included such things as requiring teachers to wash windows once a week and check the outhouses daily. Women were not permitted to wear the following apparel in public: skirts slit to expose ankles (that's right, ankles), a bathing costume, or bloomers for cycling. Men were not allowed to wear shirt sleeves unlinked and rolled, hair closely cropped (unless bald or having a disease of the scalp), or detachable collar and neck tie removed from shirt. It sounds like someone might have made up these rules, but I remember when ladies were not permitted to wear shorts downtown and members of different genders did not use the same swimming facilities at church camp.

A plaque on my wall at home includes rules that you would think a comedian made up. These rules are highly entertaining, but if you talk to many teachers you will discover that some of the things teachers are asked to do today are just as silly. Following is a reproduction of the rules on the plaque:

RULES FOR TEACHERS
1872

1. Teachers each day will fill lamps and clean chimneys.
2. Each teacher will bring a bucket of water and a scuttle of coal for the day's session.
3. Make your pens carefully. You may whittle nibs to the individual taste of your pupils.
4. Men teachers may take one evening each week for courting purposes, or two evenings a week if they go to church regularly.
5. After ten hours in school, the teachers may spend the remaining time reading the Bible or other good books.
6. Women teachers who marry or engage in unseemly conduct will be dismissed.

7. Every teacher should lay aside from each pay a goodly sum of his earnings for his benefit during his declining years so that he will not become a burden on society.

8. Any teacher who smokes, uses liquor in any form, frequents pool or public halls, or gets shaved in a barber shop will give good reason to suspect his worth, intention, integrity and honesty.

9. The teacher who performs his labor faithfully and without fault for five years will be given an increase of twenty-five cents per week in his pay, providing the Board of Education approves.

A few years ago I thought it would be fun to write a parody of those rules as they related to Stanislaus School and the teachers and conditions here at that time. Here is that list with explanations in parenthesis where necessary:

RULES FOR TEACHERS
1985

1. Teachers will locate the breaker box closest to their classroom and learn to reset switches when the power fails in their room. (Our school needs repowering— not enough electricity to run the place!)

2. Teachers will clean the cobwebs from corners of the classroom so that children will not be frightened. They will check for and kill any red ants before children arrive each morning so that the ants do not eat children's lunches.

3. Each teacher will feel the floor with an ungloved hand to determine if the heat is on and will report promptly to the principal in the event water begins spouting from the floor. (I told you it was an old school. The furnace heats water which flows through copper tubing which runs under the tile flooring. Tile is laid on

top of a concrete floor which occasionally cracks. If a joint in the copper tubing breaks, water seeks an outlet and sometimes seeps through cracks and floods a room. Oh, it is great fun!)

4. Teachers will sharpen pencils carefully, encourage children to reuse facial tissue and use the back side of photocopy paper. In the event that teachers run short of pencils, they are encouraged to borrow from students who buy by volume from the pencil machine. Further, there will be no more Kleenex when the twelve cases ordered in September are depleted. No more photocopy paper will be ordered when the machine reading exceeds one million copies or when the 240 cases of paper furnished by the governing board for model, "paper curriculum" schools has run out.

5. Men teachers who are married, must show no evidence of being henpecked (two calls from spouse in one day = henpecked), speak up at faculty meetings where they are greatly out-numbered, and take their turn cleaning the Staff Room without being reminded by female employees.

6. Any teacher who spends ten hours on any given day at school may ask the principal for release time on Friday provided lesson plans are turned in, papers graded, and the classroom is neat and tidy.

7. Women teachers who do not parallel park correctly will be directed to park in the east parking lot. A written reprimand will be placed in the teacher's personnel file if she fails to leave the twelve to fifteen inches prescribed between the curb and the car. There must also be thirty-six inches between the car in front and the car at the rear. Male teachers, who are proficient at parallel parking, may earn one hour of release time by providing parking instruction to

female teachers.

8. Every teacher will pay a minimum of thirty percent of his pay warrant for state and federal taxes, one-fifth of his pay for fringe benefits, and fifteen percent for retirement purposes. Teachers are encouraged to budget the remainder of their pay wisely, recognizing that they will receive no pay during the summer months.

9. Teachers are not to eat out more than twice a month, and then only at fast food places, and are not to ask the secretary to cash their personal checks for more than $5.00 more than once a month.

10. Any teacher who spends all recesses in the Staff Room drinking coffee or cokes, leaves the campus at noontime, attends regular Friday "seminars" at Garcia's, or smokes a pipe in the restroom, will give good cause for the principal to suspect his sanity.

11. The teacher who survives in the profession for forty years will be recommended to the governing board for a certificate of merit (suitable for framing, but the frame is not provided) and may, upon the completion of the fortieth year opt to receive a retirement bonus of $5,000 provided he/she is willing to write two special projects for the district and substitute upon demand for one school year.

Finding good teachers is not easy. When you do find them, the competition is so keen, it is difficult to draw them to your school and/or district. A few years ago I offered a fourth grade position to one of the candidates who had scored high in our interview process. She came to school and met with me to look over the facilities. She interviewed me at that time. Then she said she needed more time to decide. A few days later I called to inquire about her decision. She informed me that she had decided to sign a contract with another district.

The colleges and universities are doing a much better job of training teachers now. Our local university (University of California, Stanislaus) has an excellent teacher training program. Local administrators work in conjunction with college professors at the Education Department's invitation, to screen candidates who would like to enter the teacher training program. These three-person teams conduct formal interviews of candidates, complete evaluation forms, and make recommendations about the candidate's potential. A candidate has completed four years of college work at this point, and if accepted into the program, will enter the fifth year of schooling which will include student teaching.

Many school districts in the area have agreements with the university to place student teachers at their schools. A student teacher is assigned to a master teacher at two different schools and two different levels. For instance, a student teacher will work with a sixth grade master teacher one semester and then move to another school to work with a first grade teacher. The student teacher begins the experience by observing the master teacher, meets to discuss issues, learns how to write lesson plans and implement them, and meets regularly with a university supervisor. A master teacher receives the whopping sum of $100 for working with a student teacher. This is a valuable experience for student teachers, and most worthwhile for the master teacher if the student is competent. A master teacher is one who is tenured—has successfully taught for more than two years. The student teacher provides another set of hands! Once in a great while a not-so-competent student teacher comes along who needs a lot of extra help to make it. Student teachers are not assigned to probationary teachers. While a teacher may choose not to be assigned a student teacher because they require a great deal of work, most master teachers enjoy working with them because they provide fresh new ideas, are teachable, and possess a fresh enthusiasm for teaching.

For a ten-year period of time our district elementary interview team was invited to the university to conduct "mock interviews" for the Education Department. The students in the class were completing their fifth year and had already received training on how to prepare their resumes. Four principals from my district conducted the mock interview in the same manner we would use to interview a candidate for a job in our district. A "brave" student volunteered (on the spot usually) to serve as the "guinea pig." The candidate was invited in for the interview and made to feel welcome and comfortable with small talk before we began the questioning process. Each of us asked our favorite questions dealing with discipline, the curriculum, setting up reading groups, and information about the candidate's prior experience, interests, and grade level preferences. One of my favorite questions is: "On a scale from one to ten with ten being the highest, rate yourself on energy, initiative, and organization (the E.I.O. test)." Interviewees enjoy answering this question, and it provides some valuable insights for interviewers.

The very first time the interview team visited an education class to conduct a mock interview, we met with some hostility. After interviewing a candidate, each of us used the rating sheet. The points were calculated and divided by four (number on the interview team) to arrive at the final ranking. When I announced a score in the mid-eighties, I could feel the negative vibes emanating from the audience. I quickly explained that the candidate's score was respectable, and she would probably be on our list to hire if she did as well on a real interview for a position in the district. Candidates must score seventy points or better in order to qualify for a position on an eligibility list. It is rather uncommon for a candidate to receive more than ninety points when we average our four scores, but it has happened a number of times. We proceeded to critique the mock interview, fielded questions from both the candidate and the audience, and offered suggestions to candidates about ways to prepare for an interview. Over the last few years, we have hired several students who participated in these mock interviews. Conducting these mock interviews is a rewarding experience both for the students and for our district.

During my career so far I have interviewed literally hundreds of teachers. God has given each of us certain talents and while I sometimes have trouble knowing whether I have one at all, selecting teachers comes close. I greatly enjoy the interview process and am able to recognize a "top" teacher quickly. An interview takes approximately twenty minutes, but you really do not need that long to recognize the potential of a candidate. By board policy our interview team is also required to observe each candidate while he or she is teaching a lesson. If the candidate is not already teaching, we invite him to one of our schools to teach a lesson on any subject he chooses.

Sometimes it is difficult to arrange for a candidate to observe. One year the team had to go through the interview process several times. It was the end of June before we completed the task. During the final phase of interviewing, the district summer session was in progress. Often we invite a candidate to teach a lesson during summer school by taking over a summer school teacher's classroom. We asked one candidate if she would mind preparing a lesson and presenting it to us in this way. The directions were not clearly given! When the candidate came to present the lesson, she was under the impression that she would be teaching the lesson to us four principals—not to a class. I was greatly relieved when the lesson was over and we were able to get up off the carpet. She had prepared a lesson for kindergarten children. We principals played the role of kindergarten children.

We call former employers to check references on each candidate. We, the interview team, have an agreement among ourselves that we will not qualify a candidate for a teaching position if we would not want that person at our school. After all, the candidate may be transferred to other school sites some time in the future.

A more thorough education is being provided for teacher candidates by our colleges and universities. Candidates for teaching positions need training regarding proper interviewing techniques. One of the clearest messages a candidate should be given is that during the interview process he is "selling himself." Confidence and a lack of nervousness must shine through. Interview teams look for teachers who have had experience working with children and who have a genuine love for them. It is important for the candidate to practice or do mock interviews. Questions the interview team may asked need to be anticipated. Dressing appropriately but not overdoing it is important. I don't necessarily expect a teacher candidate to wear a suit when it is over one hundred degrees outside. Knowledge of curriculum is crucial, but candidate's answers should not sound like they are coming from "the book." A good sense of humor is useful. Finally, working with others is crucial. The candidate needs to give careful attention when answering questions dealing with authority and relationships.

Interviewing teachers is an awesome responsibility. If the interview team does a good job of gathering and evaluating information about candidates, it will have a much higher degree of success in choosing teachers who will be effective in the classroom. I would much rather allocate more time to the interview process than go through the steps necessary to dismiss an inadequate teacher later on. Districts need to be cautious about making the interview team too large. Applicants are nervous enough without having to face eight or ten persons on an interview team. When my district opened its sixth school, administrators were divided into two teams. Some districts choose to seat a teacher and a parent on their teams. Team members are generally assigned questions to ask. In order to be fair, each member of the team needs to ask each candidate the same question. Interview teams do not need to be cold and calculating. Competition is keen, and we want the best teachers. But achieving this goal does not give us license to treat applicants we interview harshly. If we have done a good job of screening candidates, the interview process will go smoothly.

There has only been one occasion since I have been interviewing that a teacher was employed who did not do a satisfactory job. Much time and money is actually saved by districts that do a quality job of interviewing and selecting new staff. Teachers can be dismissed, but it is a tedious, time-consuming task and not very pleasant for all concerned. Even though this teacher had a wealth of experience in the subject area, came with good references, and taught an acceptable lesson the interview team was fooled. Other members of the team felt the person would be great. I had some strong reservations, but did not voice them loudly enough. The teacher was dismissed after the first year.

While interviewing teachers is a tiring job, there are some funny moments when it takes all the restraint I can muster to keep from "cracking up." One time we interviewed a teacher whom we as the interview team affectionately remember as "the singing interviewee." We asked our usual questions, and at some point in the interview this candidate, who could talk a mile a minute, began singing a song. She was dead serious! She finished the verse (I really thought she was going to ask us to join her for verse two) and kept talking without missing a beat. We were not especially looking for a soloist.

Some candidates literally talk themselves out of a job. It's best to answer the questions as clearly and succinctly as possible. If the team wants more information, let them ask. Other qualities I look for in a candidate include: self confidence, good sense of humor (rarely does this come out in an interview), knowledge of curriculum without sounding like the answers are coming from a textbook, and a feeling that the candidate really loves and enjoys working with children (This quality is usually apparent when the candidates are observed).

Another vital link in the process of educating children is the substitute "pool." It is difficult to find quality substitute teachers. Fortunately in my district principals are not responsible for arranging for substitute teachers. The district contracts with the county schools office for this service. A teacher calls the substitute teacher placement office to request a substitute. When the district conducts teacher training sessions, substitutes are arranged en masse by the central office. When a large number of teachers is out at one time, some of the substitutes sent out by the county are not the best.

One afternoon after school had been dismissed, a substitute assigned to Stanislaus rushed into the office and asked to use the telephone. He called someone and asked that they bring out the "extra set of car keys." Okay, so what's the big deal? We all lock our keys in the car once in awhile. Well, it turned out that this fellow not only locked the keys in the car, but he left them in the ignition with the motor running. The car had been running all day and was still going strong when someone arrived with the extra set of keys. That experience would win an award to go with the statement: "You know it's a bad day when . . . ."

Hiring the very best teachers will make your life as a principal much easier. I care enough to hire the very best!

14

TEACHERS HAVE CLASS

One of my favorite bumper stickers displays the words:

"If you can read this message, thank a teacher."

Each year in California a state proclamation declares a special day to honor teachers. "The Day of the Teacher," as it is known, occurs in the month of May. The Stanislaus School Student Council creatively devotes much energy toward planning events to honor teachers on their day. For example, the Council's favorite activity includes taking the teachers out for breakfast. Since our Student Council has separate officers and representatives for each semester during the school year, it is an easy task to assign students to host special teachers like the band director, Resource Specialist, art teacher, kindergarten teachers, and teachers in grades K through two who do not have council representatives. The room representatives at each grade level are responsible for creating place mats, coordinating a class greeting card with everyone in the classroom signing it, sitting with their teacher, and serving as the teacher's aide for the day. This activity has been done both at school in our cafeteria and at local restaurants. When we have had breakfast at school, council members decorated the cafeteria and served the food to their teachers. No wonder they prefer going to a restaurant. They don't have to work as hard!

One year skits were prepared with representatives from each classroom deciding how they would feature their teacher. Some students chose funny skits depicting teacher's mannerisms or expressions their teacher used over and over. Other students chose a more serious approach by writing a poem or composing an essay praising their teacher. Council members performed their skits at an all-school assembly. We usually have separate primary and intermediate assemblies, but on rare occasions like this we all squeeze into the cafeteria.

Last year we nearly had a stampede on "The Day of the Teacher." Council members had decided (in a rare moment of insanity, I gave them the idea!) to have a fire drill about thirty minutes before the end of the school day. When all of the classes had egressed to their routine, appointed fire drill positions, a council member was to come to the front of each line, yell, "Charge! We love our teachers!" and dash for the cafeteria. Word was supposed to have been spread around the campus at noon via the room representatives so that only students would know what was happening. Once inside the cafeteria, students were supposed to sit down and remain absolutely quiet until the teachers arrived. Well, we did arrive in the cafeteria and teachers did come in very confused (and a few told me later they were ready to "chew their class out"). The plan fell apart, however, because many of the students did not know what was happening. Communication is so important!

We had planned to have an assembly to honor the teachers, but the students were so loud that I could not project over the noise with the volume on the PA turned up full blast. By the time order and quiet were restored, we had time to display the huge banner (STANISLAUS TEACHERS HAVE CLASS) which was held by council members across the front of the cafeteria, say a few words of praise, and it was time for students to be dismissed. So, we didn't get to sing the song I made up. I think it was a conspiracy from the beginning—the Council wasn't very enthused about my song. I don't know why that was—it sounded good to me. The first line started with, "We love our teachers; Oh, yes, we do . . . ." I will spare you the rest! I guess it all turned out for the best. At least we had done other things that day and during the week to honor the teachers. Each day of the week beginning on Monday, council members had been assigned tasks to complete which would honor the teachers. For example, a large red apple was placed on each teacher's desk on Monday, a card signed by all class members was presented on Tuesday, students wrote an essay about their teacher on Wednesday, and a large cake was delivered for them to consume on Thursday. You know about Friday!

When I was a student at Baylor University in Waco, Texas, I worked at a hamburger place called WHAT-A-BURGER. I had never heard of such a place before I began working there, but could they make hamburgers! We literally built hamburgers, and we built them fast. Everyone had his job to do. One person manned the grille, one was in charge of buns (mustard, mayonnaise), one stacked the tomatoes, lettuce, and pickles, and one handled drinks and the cash register. What an operation! Those were the best hamburgers I have ever eaten. The manager always told us to build a burger like we were going to eat it ourselves. That would make a difference, wouldn't it? What does this story have to do with being a principal or with teachers? Just this.

To me building a staff is somewhat analogous to building a hamburger. I related earlier in the book that when I came to Stanislaus School as a principal, there were thirteen teachers on staff and nine of them were approaching retirement age. I had an opportunity to build a new staff over the next few years. Fortunately, not all of those veteran teachers retired the same year. That would have been a disaster. It would be like a football team with all rookies. The veteran teachers worked with the new ones by sharing discipline ideas, curriculum projects, and other things from their "bag of tricks." Every teacher must develop a "bag of tricks" (defined as gimmicks and various ways and means to control children and actively involve them in the learning process).

As our team of principals interviewed each spring, I had a clear image of the teaching positions which would be open at my school. By maintaining a low profile (and with a little wheeling and dealing, I must admit) I was able to convince the other members of the interview team that certain candidates would work very nicely at my school. Besides, in those days the district was not growing by ten percent each year, and just about the only new teachers needed were to replace those who were retiring. I'm not saying that I got the candidates at the top of the list with the most points each year, but I secured ones who would be compatible with my staff, the parents in the community, and the students who attend the school. There is not a teacher on staff that I would be hesitant to have as a teacher for my own children.

Only two of the original teachers who were at Stanislaus when I started remain today. Both are men who have chosen to remain at grades one and four for the duration. With increased growth there has also been an increase in staff reaching a high of twenty-three teachers. I wanted a good balance, with men teaching throughout the grades. Only kindergarten and grade three do not have a male teacher this year. Unfortunately, some of the teachers I hired decided to stop teaching to start their own families. I lost some really great teachers to motherhood. As a district we have always tried to find the very best teachers. Some districts do not hire teachers with many years of experience because their salaries will be higher than inexperienced teachers just beginning their careers. As an example of this practice, I remember a junior high English teacher we hired who had his doctorate. He had just returned from a two-year teaching assignment in Australia, had excellent references, and was offered a contract. Later he became the district's first curriculum director.

So, I have built a strong staff of teachers. These teachers work together as a team. For the most part, I think they would carry on just fine without me. But then, who would attend all the district meetings and do all of the paper work? Having three teachers at each grade level is ideal. Teachers get together (we call these sessions grade level meetings), sometimes weekly, to discuss problems, analyze test scores, develop curriculum, plan field trips, and just to share ideas and strategies. They enjoy being together as a faculty. Many faculty lounges are very negative places where gossip flows and demeaning remarks are made about students. That is certainly not the case in the lounge at Stanislaus School.

Working with a team of dedicated teachers is a rewarding experience. California implemented a mentor teacher program several years ago. These are teachers who are recognized by their peers and selected by the governing board to receive this special honor. The position also pays the recipient an extra $4000 a year. A mentor teacher in my district works with new teachers, develops curriculum standards, models effective teaching practices, or works on projects as directed by the curriculum director. One of my teachers was selected as the first mentor teacher in the school district. Since then two other teachers have been so honored. One teacher on this staff was selected as the outstanding educator in the county and did quite well in the state competition. Teachers on this staff work on many district committees during the school year, and some of them work on curriculum projects during the summer months. All of this translates into a better education for children.

I expect teachers to be positive rather than negative with

children in their classrooms. Many of them have a rule which states, "No put-downs." They recognize and reward children who are performing well. They use effective teaching techniques to insure that each child in the room has an equal opportunity to learn. I want teachers to be firm, fair, and consistent when working with children. Teachers need to be patient, caring, and understanding. I don't think it is too much to ask for them to be sensitive to the needs of each child in the classroom. Some children are tough and will not mind or work without a firm, no- nonsense approach. Other children need lots of TLC (tender loving care). There are ever-increasing numbers of children from broken homes, from minority groups who speak little or no English, or from homes in our area where both parents work full time (some commuting to the San Francisco Bay area which is one hundred miles away) and have little time for the children. Teachers are expected to meet the diverse needs of all of these youngsters. The task simply cannot be done by teachers who do not love what they are doing and who do not really care for children.

If I expect my teachers to perform in certain ways, I believe they have a right to expect certain behaviors of me also. All of us enjoy receiving a pat on the back. It is pleasant to hear someone say, "Thank you. You are doing a nice job." On the other hand, it is not pleasant to work for someone who is stingy with compliments. Everyone needs to be encouraged regularly. Principals can do a great deal to build self confidence in a teacher by his attitude on the job. I do not "put down" teachers—especially in front of peers. Being "chewed out" by the boss in a faculty meeting is uncalled for and unprofessional. But it happens. Teachers are going to make mistakes. We all do. It is important to recognize what you did wrong and work to correct it. But the principal can deliver that message without being the "bad guy." On teacher evaluations I try to be completely positive. If one or two negative points are written in an evaluation, the teacher will many times fail to see the good things that were said. It is much wiser to point out the negative things you would like to see improved when you meet with the teacher to go over the evaluation.

One of the things I love most about my job is visiting classrooms. It is such a treat to walk into a classroom where effective teaching is occurring. Teachers enjoy receiving a note in their mailbox that lets them know the principal was impressed by what he observed. This year I learned a new trick at a conference I attended. I carry a "stick-em" pad with me into a room, write a brief note after a short visit, and leave it on the teacher's desk on my way out. The first time I did this, several teachers told me that they rushed right over to see what I had placed on their desk. For the past several years during the month of January (because it is so BLAH) I have placed large red apples on teachers' desks before they arrived at school. This inexpensive treat brightens the teachers' day and let's them know I care. I maintain a log of my visits to the classrooms which contains dates, times, and what I observed when I visited. I record official evaluation dates, times when I have left a note on the teacher's desk, and times when I have written a longer note to place in the teacher's mailbox. This log is valuable to me because it helps me track which rooms I am not visiting as often as I should. For example, the afternoon kindergarten is often slighted due to the number of afternoon meetings I must attend. As I have mentioned before, the first wing of our school has a long hallway. One of the things I have done to honor teachers and staff was to mount each one of their pictures in the hallway. Above the pictures, a large computer-made banner proclaimed "WALL OF FAME"

One of the newest movements in the field of education is called "Teacher Empowerment." Teachers all around the country are demanding more of a voice in what happens at their schools. Some principals are afraid that this movement will strip them of their power. As long as I have some control over the staff that works at my school (hiring and transfers), teacher empowerment does not bother me. I think more heads make for better decisions. There was a time when top administrators probably had more knowledge about happenings around the school. That is not necessarily true today. Some positions in the central office require specialists (finance, school building projects, and educational law to name a few), just like in other professions, but teachers today are working with children and with curriculum and need a stronger say regarding what works and what doesn't work. My former superintendent maintained that "he who has the most knowledge should make the decisions." My teachers exemplify very high professional standards, and I know that decisions we make together provide the children we serve with better educational opportunities. Only an unwise administrator would make decisions that affect teachers and children without the support and cooperation of these professionals who are "on the firing line" day after day.

When I first came to Stanislaus, many schools were beginning school improvement programs. This program provided schools with additional funds based on average daily attendance. For Stanislaus the dollar amount would have been approximately $35,000 at the time. I could have decided that we would become involved, and that would have been that. However, I brought the idea to the staff and to the parents group for discussion. The parents group unanimously endorsed the idea. The faculty voted it down. A few years later when the district hired a new superintendent, the decision was made for us. The decision was not right for the time. A few years later with almost a totally new staff it was relatively easy to implement a school improvement program. Teachers and parents readily accepted the idea.

Without going into an exhaustive report of the activities

and projects of my teachers, I would like to share some memorable ones which might give you an idea or two. When the school had a much smaller enrollment, one of the fifth grade teachers and her class decided to sell things such as popcorn (unpopped, in small bags) to raise money for starving children in Ethiopia. The project was presented to me by the teacher, and it sounded like a fine idea. Plans were made to invite the local newspaper to cover the story, but then we always call the newspaper and, of course, they can't cover everything. This one they did cover! The teacher invited Gary Condit, our area assemblyman, to school. Mr. Condit has moved on to Washington, D.C. where he serves us in Congress. I will never forget the day Mr. Condit and his aide arrived at Stanislaus School. Like many projects, I thought this one was low key. You know, collect a few bags of popcorn, sell them, and send a check for a few dollars to help some starving kids. Mr. Condit arrived with his shirt sleeves rolled up, carrying a large case of popcorn (and there was more). He spent the afternoon with that class. Everyone had to have his autograph and a picture taken with him. Children (and all of the adults present) were permitted to ask him questions just like a presidential news conference.

Each year the Jaycees sponsor a shopping spree for needy children in our area. Schools submit names of children who are then paired with volunteers to go shopping for clothing. Approximately $100 is spent on each child. Following the shopping spree, children visit with Santa and enjoy a Christmas party. Children come to school the next day all dressed up in their new clothes. It's quite a sight! Many of the teachers give their time to take children shopping. This year, in addition, four teachers worked with local agencies on the "adopt a family" program. Teachers and children gathered toys, food, clothing, and other items for "their family." Families remained anonymous and did not have children at our school. One first grade teacher and his students decided to collect stuffed animals to give to needy children. Children had been bringing stuffed animals for show and tell. As Christmas time approached, there was a discussion about all the children who had no teddy bear to cuddle with each night. With parents' permission, children brought all kinds of stuffed animals. I have never seen such a collection. They were all over the room. Other classes were invited to join in bringing their discarded stuffed animals. Some of these stuffed animals found their way into the Christmas baskets being prepared for the classes participating in the "adopt a family program."

Teachers have done all of the standard things like celebrating the one hundredth day of school, inviting local radio DJs to come to school to interview students at election time on how they would vote (if they could), plant gardens, conduct wind and weather experiments, launch rockets, have pen pals sharing videos and letters across the states and in foreign countries, launch balloons with notes attached to see which one would go farthest, whole class baking projects (the apple pies were the best!), cooking solar hot dogs, having Smokey Bear at school to talk about fire safety and Freddy Frog to talk about water safety, celebrating "teddy bear" day in the kindergarten, having our own national election, dissecting a cow (it was legal then), having the sheriff's deputies demonstrate horseback-riding techniques, demonstrations by police canines, kindergarten sleep-ins, and taking field trips all over northern California. Once a teacher was able to "pull the right strings" to get a local hospital to land their helicopter, which is used for rescue operations, on our playground. We kept a safe distance until it landed and then everyone gathered around to learn about this interesting vocation. These are just a few of the activities teachers have used to motivate children in conjunction with units or projects being done.

A few years ago we started a cross-aged tutoring program which has been very successful. Teachers in lower grades request assistance from fifth and sixth grade students. These students are paired with one or two children to drill them on math facts or reading vocabulary. Some of the sixth grade teachers have students complete a job application, provide references (secretary, principal, etc.), and interview with the teacher they will work for in the lower grades. Students also earn Kool Aide points for serving their school as a tutor. Teachers select students (not just the top ones) who will benefit from this experience. Some of the best success stories come from low-achieving children. The fifth grade classes have traditionally joined with primary classes for a "buddy" program. Each fifth grader is paired with a second grader, and on given days during the year, teachers plan projects such as having children read to each other or complete creative writing activities.

One of the most frustrating things for a teacher to deal with is having a student he does not know how to handle, either because of behavior problems or academic concerns, and having no place to go for help. Through our School Improvement Program we formed a Child Study Team composed of one primary and one intermediate teacher, the Resource Specialist, principal, and the teacher making the referral. The team meets regularly because teachers have come to respect the assistance their peers provide at these meetings. I am amazed at the depth of perception and caring these people share. As a result of these meetings, children have been referred for medical examinations where hearing or sight problems were diagnosed and corrected, for special help through our resource program in math or reading, and even for special day class which completely removes the child from mainstream, regular education. The meetings last well beyond the teachers' regular work day.

I suppose every principal feels he has the best teachers on his staff, and that's as it should be. I spend many Saturday mornings working at school, and on many of these days (and some holidays) there are enough teachers working to conduct a faculty meeting. It is sad (and discouraging) that so many people in the United States know so little about the role of teachers. There is enough ignorance out there to fill another book! Contrary to what many people believe, teachers work more than six hours a day. They spend evenings and weekends preparing lessons and correcting papers. If teachers charged for all of the "extra" things they do for children (like lawyers, doctors, plumbers, and tax preparers do), stop and think about what that monthly bill would be like! Teaching requires more energy and creativity than most professions I know. Teachers are constantly on stage. Considering the large salaries in many other fields of work today and the lack of respect by the public at large, it is a wonder so many teachers remain. Teachers are overworked and underpaid, but that has forever been the case in our country. Teachers stay, teachers teach, and teachers work hard because they love children and want to make a difference in their lives.

15

LET THERE BE PRAISE

A song by Sandi Patti, one of the popular Christian vocalists today, titled "LET THERE BE PRAISE" dwells on my mind at times when I am out on the playground—especially after we have practiced it at choir rehearsal or sung it on Sunday. I like to think of the first line "Let there be praise, let there be joy in my heart" as a prayer that God will help me to be a joyful person all through the day. On some days it is easier to be joyful than others. It is so rewarding to work with children and feel as if you have accomplished something.

One of our intermediate students has more athletic ability than any student I have ever known. He is a natural athlete. There is only one problem. He will not accept discipline. On those rare occasions when he would listen, I have tried to help him realize that he needs discipline in his life to be successful. It matters not how much talent he has if he is unable to discipline himself. He constantly blames other people for his difficulty when he is sent to the office. He will never admit his own guilt or take responsibility for his actions. I can't help him, and he can't help himself until he is willing to admit that he needs help. He thinks everyone picks on him, and that life isn't fair, although he didn't express it in those exact words. There's a good kid in there somewhere—a real winner. I would like to read about his successes in sports in the newspaper in years to come. It is a humbling experience for me to work with young people with so much talent.

Many children learn and succeed despite what we as educators do, but many succeed because of dedicated teachers who literally pour their lives into them. I have been at my present school long enough to see kindergartners go all the way through high school. Many of them achieve honors throughout their school careers. Others have graduated from college and are being successful in their chosen careers. Students I taught have children who attend my school. Two of my former students are teachers in the district.

All of the children do not make it. That is hard to deal with. My faith was really tested a few years ago when one of our fourth grade boys died. This very popular young man had attended Stanislaus since kindergarten, was a good student, served on the Student Council in grade three, and was very athletic. He fought a losing battle with leukemia. An evergreen tree planted on our campus serves as a memorial to this student who lived courageously and set such a good example for his peers. Last year the Student Council voted to dedicate the yearbook to him. Losing one of your students hurts deeply—it's like losing one of your own children.

Some of the children don't turn out the way you hope they would. One boy who went through Stanislaus always tried to buy "friends." He alienated his peers by this and other behaviors. One thing led to another, and this young man is in prison where he will probably spend the rest of his life. You can see them developing wrong values and attitudes from the time they enter kindergarten. When they will not accept help, what can you do!

Every principal and teacher can relate special stories about children who attended their school or were in their class. All of the children are special, and God has a special plan for each one of them. It's tough to see children suffer and experience pain. One time a little kindergarten boy with diabetes went into shock. He was unconscious. His teacher cuddled him in her arms as we waited for the paramedics to arrive to transport him to the hospital. I admire the courage of the first grade boy suffering from multiple sclerosis who wanted to remain in the regular school setting rather than attend a special school. He was chosen to be the "Poster Boy" for Stanislaus County. Seeing him fall on the playground so many times and labor valiantly to get up brought tears to my eyes.

Many students do special things for you. Children in one family have almost single-handedly outfitted me for all the holidays. A Santa tie with a bright red nose, Christmas tree suspenders, snowman socks, "Be My Valentine" socks, mugs, and baseball caps are part of that collection. one of my favorite gifts came from a sixth grade girl who made mugs for her teacher, the secretary and myself. What made these ceramic mugs so special, besides the fact that they were handmade, was that the girl had captured each of us in an unforgetable pose. A kindergarten class presented me with a book entitled *THOMAS' SNOWSUIT* after I read a story to them. Another kindergarten class came to the office on Valentine's Day, sang us a song, and gave the secretaries and me large construction paper envelopes filled with valentines. Another memorable event occurred on my birthday one year when every child in the school came snaking (like coming in one door and going out the other) through the office singing happy birthday to me. One morning I came to work and the message on the large marquee in front of school read, "The Best Boss Bosses Here!" I have filing cabinet drawers full of cards, stories, and other things children and teachers have given me over the years. The point of all this is that there are "bouquets," there are rewards, and parents, teachers, and children do care and let you know it when you are doing a good job.

I would like to share one special letter written by a former student who is now attending Harvard.

Dear Mr. Datsun, (. . . they sometimes get it right!)

Thank you so much for everything you have done for me and our whole school.

I'll really hate to leave Stanislaus. I'll really miss it. No other principal:

1. Had Student Council
2. Had Student of the Week and Month
3. Took us to lunch and Beard Brook Park
4. Had parties like skating and bowling
5. Was as easy to talk to.

All of the kids really think you are neat—they're right! You are really super, and without you the school year would not be as fun-filled.

Hope you have a great summer vacation.

I think you have found the secret to being a great principal. For one thing, you treat sixth graders like they are at least a little mature—not like second graders. You really know how to make people feel good inside and a little more respected.

I had a real super year, and to tell you the truth, I sort of wish it hadn't ended.

> Respectfully submitted, (Ha! Ha!)
> Merry Read
> Student Council President

All of those memories are special, and I'm thankful for the love, consideration, and support expressed by my staff, parents, and students.

The principal makes a big difference at school. His behavior affects the teachers who in turn affect the students. Teachers are on stage for their students, and principals are on stage for the entire community which includes staff, teachers, parents, children and the district office. Sounds like an impossible job. It really is if you try to do it alone! The principal sets the tone for the school as this poem relates:

THE PRINCIPAL

What a difference the principal makes at school!
It's his domain—his place to rule.
The principal is boss and leader and friend;
A person teachers confide in;
A person who is determined to win.
Parents expect a miracle man;
And kids—to get away with as much as they can.

Secretaries wish he would slow down.
The VP would like for him to transfer uptown.
Superintendents expect reports on time,
And the budget balanced to the last dime.
Custodians know the place must be clean
With nary a spider web and no dust to be seen.
Teachers are alarmed when his door is closed;
He's talking about them, or so they suppose.
The bus driver wants him to come aboard
With a passioned plea that can't be ignored.
He works closely with the PTA;
Attends board meetings for no extra pay.

He is fair and consistent and firm as can be
At settling quarrels and squabbles singlehandedly.
Meeting goals and objectives requires much work,
So let the coffee continue to perk.
Curriculum and frameworks must be aligned,
And teachers evaluated before new contracts are signed.

There are conferences to attend and meetings galore;
Irate parents, he cannot ignore!
As much as he'd love to have a nice day—
Conflicts arise that won't go away!
It would be easy to quit—find something more lucrative
    to do;
But precious moments occur, though sometimes they're
    few.
A friendly little face
Comes rushing at a fast pace,
With a hug to share,
And at once you're aware
That God has given to you
A great opportunity, and a job shared by very few.

So, Mr. Principal, do your best;
Your reward will be better than you could ever guess.

EPILOGUE

"Into, Through, and Beyond" are new catch words being bandied around in conjunction with the whole language approach to reading in California these days. Children get a feel for journeying "INTO" the literature with a broad range of background building activities, going "THROUGH" the literature by reading and enjoying the stories, and exploring "BEYOND" the literature with writing, performing, and discussion activities.

I have attempted to take you on a journey "INTO" the world of the elementary school principal. No two days are ever remotely the same, and the "surprises" I encounter, which would have constituted colossal happenings a few years ago, become so routine that I hardly miss a beat anymore. Children are always the same, but yet always different. Problems are different, and yet even they seem always the same. But, the children will forever be special and unique. They are the reason this job is so special.

I have taken you "THROUGH" good times and bad times at Stanislaus Union Elementary School. We have not arrived. There is much room for improvement. But we are making progress. The school is a friendly place today with a student body that makes me proud. Children have their differences. They will always need help untangling their little webs of entanglement. But, basically they get along very well. Allow me to share two final stories to illustrate the point.

Sandi and Polly are super good friends and have been for a couple of years. Both girls are very strong willed, and when a new girl enrolled in their class and Polly wanted to be best friends with her, it created the typical jealousy syndrome in Sandi. The rivalry went the rounds with quarrels, abusive telephone calls, upset parents, gossiping and cutting remarks occurring without end. I became involved when one of the mothers called to ask if there was anything I could do. Her daughter was so upset that she no longer wanted to come to school. In our lengthy counseling sessions, both girls openly shared their feelings. They really wanted to be friends. At this point, having involved their parents who were justifiably angry with the whole situation, they didn't know what to do. Over a period of days, we spent several hours talking things through. Both parents separately felt it would be best if the girls stayed away from each other for awhile. I thought the girls had made tremendous progress (if tears are any indication, but then I'm a softie!), but they agreed to play with other friends and give each other some "space." A few days later they came into my office with their arms around each other and announced that they didn't need any more space. They were fast friends, and everything was well with the world.

Perry, a small black boy in a combination first/second grade class, had his cookie grabbed out of his hand by a much larger second grader named Johnny who was also in his class. It was snack recess, and Johnny had volunteered several times to help Perry eat his cookie. When Perry refused the fourth time, Johnny grabbed the cookie and gobbled it down. Well, the two were sent to see the principal. Upon investigating the "Cookie Caper," I discovered that Johnny had not brought a snack that day. He also had not eaten breakfast. As he sat right next to Perry with tears in his eyes, he reached over and put his hand on Perry's shoulder and said, "I'm sorry I took your cookie." He agreed to make restitution by buying Perry an ice cream on Friday. Both boys walked out of my office with their arms around each other. What a sight!

There is a great deal of camaraderie among the staff members at Stanislaus School. Teachers openly share ideas, exchange yard duties, and enjoy each other's company in the Staff Lounge. We share secret pals, celebrate all the birthdays, have good old-fashioned, potluck lunches, and joke around like a bunch of children. It is my personal belief that the office staff (they will no doubt file a grievance over this statement!) spearheads the various and sundry activities which produce the hilarious laughter heard frequently in the hallway.

Parents love this old school. When the governing board was considering changing the school district attendance boundaries because of the addition of a new school, many of the parents were more than a little apprehensive about sending their children to Stanislaus School. There were rumors about the cafeteria ceiling falling on children as they ate, undrinkable water, unsafe traffic problems due to the highway, and farmers spraying pesticides during school hours. Last spring we invited the children who would come to Stanislaus and their parents to attend a "Western Day" event in order to get acquainted and "scout out" the school. A western band was hired, hot dogs were served outside, and everyone had a great time. Our new parents and students now love this school. It proves once more that you can't judge a school by its buildings, just as you can't always judge a book by its cover.

The "BEYOND" is still a mystery. That is in the future. But I have a few goals I would like to achieve for this school before I leave. We had our first, three-year school review in 1989. A team of selected county teachers and administrators spent three full school days at the school reviewing every aspect of our program. The school received several commendations. Our test scores have been improving for the past few years, but we still have some hard work ahead of us in this area. If the scores had been higher, I think we would have been in line for a distinguished school award. The staff works hard and deserves the recognition. That is one of my goals—to see Stanislaus School become a California distinguished school! I will continue working to make that goal a reality.

It is questionable at this point whether the school will even exist in the future. A proposal, before the city planning commission to develop a super, six-lane expressway around Modesto to move traffic more quickly across town, will determine our fate. If this plan is approved the entire first wing, cafeteria, and maintenance facility will be demolished. At that point there won't be enough land left for a decent school. We have waited a long time for our school to be remodeled, and now once again, the plans are "on hold." Perhaps in the near future, this school will be refurbished as planned, or maybe even better, there will be a new school to take its place.